On Your Bike
in
Devon

※

Kevin Presland

COUNTRYSIDE BOOKS
NEWBURY, BERKSHIRE

COUNTRYSIDE BOOKS
3 Catherine Road
Newbury, Berkshire

To view our complete range of books,
please visit us at
www.countrysidebooks.co.uk

ISBN 1 85306 847 0

*Dedicated to those in the local Cyclists' Touring Club
with whom I have shared so many of the routes in this book,
but particularly to the late Colin Brierly, who first taught me
what it was to tour and explore.*

Photographs by the author
Designed by Graham Whiteman

Typeset by Textype, Cambridge
Produced through MRM Associates Ltd., Reading
Printed in Italy

CONTENTS

AREA MAP SHOWING THE LOCATIONS OF THE RIDES

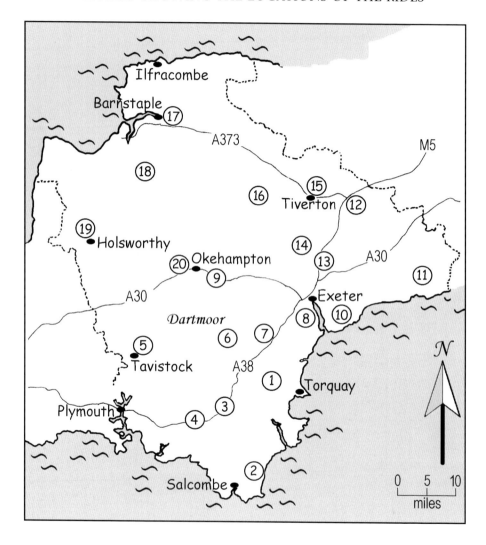

INTRODUCTION

The county of Devon offers fantastic variety, and what better way to see it than on a bicycle. Through this book I have tried to share just a little of the delight that it is to cycle here. With the greatest mileage of roads in any English county (perhaps as a consequence of having the greatest mileage of rivers), there is a tremendous choice. The opportunities to cycle are moderated a little by the hills which, without care and experience in route planning, can lead to exhausting days in the saddle. This is where this guide should prove useful.

With 24 years of experience in leading group cycle rides in Devon, the last seven of which have been with a growing family alongside, I have designed routes to avoid many of the more strenuous inclines whilst still passing places of interest. It is always useful to have an escape strategy when leading a ride, particularly when youngsters are present, and accordingly some of the rides include a shortcut back to the start.

The diversity of the county is reflected in the selection of rides. Approximately half of Devon's border is dramatic coastline, best viewed from routes 4 or 17. In addition, routes 2, 8, and 10 pass beaches at which you can stop for a paddle or swim. The best cycling in the county is probably to be found on the granite mass of Dartmoor; routes 3, 5, 6, and 9 have sections on the open moor, where you can expect to see grazing animals, rocky tors, expansive views, and beauty befitting a national park. Much of the county is rural and agricultural; on routes 1, 13, 14, 15, 16, 19, and 20 you will be in the heart of farming communities. The county has much upland in excess of 600 ft, with deep valleys carved by rivers; routes 4, 11, 12, 15, and 18 include a mixture of such river valleys and high ridges, or alternatively, just stay in the river valleys along routes 10 and 13. Historically there has been a massive investment in the south-west in the form of country homes, some of which are open to the public. Visit some examples on routes 8, 10, 11, 14, 15, and 17, and enjoy a stroll around the house and gardens and possibly a snack at the café.

For the beginner or the young family, a shortcut is available on routes 7, 8, 11, and 12. These are an ideal stepping-stone to the easy rides and, before you know it, you will be venturing out on one of the more adventurous circuits.

Kevin Presland

GUIDE TO USING THIS BOOK

Each route is preceded by information to help you:

The **number of miles** is the maximum for the ride, the distances in brackets apply if the suggested shortcuts or part routes are used. Apart from a few rides which include varying distances to be ridden on cycle tracks, all the rides are on roads with hard surfaces.

The brief **introduction** to the ride gives a broad picture of where the route goes and mentions particular features to be seen.

The **maps** listed at the beginning of each ride are all Ordnance Survey maps in the Landranger 1:50 000 series. The route could probably be followed from the description and sketch map but it is advisable to take a map as a back-up.

The **starting point** names a particular place in a village or town, together with its grid reference, and gives its location in Devon in relation to other towns or to main roads. The starting points are car parks.

Refreshments highlights the locations of tearooms or pubs. However, it is both foolish and against the law to ride under the influence of alcohol, no matter

how remote and rural the route. The location of shops is also mentioned, as a picnic can be the most enjoyable way to take lunch in the fine Devon countryside.

The route is where guidance on the nature of the roads used can be found, i.e. whether the route follows or crosses any main roads, if it is hilly, or if there are tracks to be used. Opportunities to reduce the length of the ride are described here.

Public transport details the closest accessible point by cycle-carrying public transport.

THE ROUTES

It is a good idea to read right through a route before setting out so that you can note any places where you want to spend more time. The routes have been arranged according to their position in Devon rather than their length or difficulty, so just choose ones you like the look of.

Each route is set out in numbered blocks of only a few lines, this is so that you can find your way around the page easily. The numbers correlate with those on the sketch map.

The directions have been written as clearly as possible. Instructions are given at all locations where you have to give way and at all locations where you have to turn off the major road into a minor road. Instructions are not given where you pass side roads that you are not to turn into. The turning instruction is printed in bold like this: **Turn L** at the T-junction; **fork R** at the church; **straight over** at the crossroads; first **L turning** into minor road. The name of the junction is shown in brackets. Relying on signposts can be problematic as they do get knocked down or changed; please therefore treat the signed directions with caution.

The directions include some description of places passed along the way, but at the end of each route there is more information about **places of interest.** These include notes about architecture, history, legends, the natural landscape and people.

The map of Devon on page 4 shows where the routes are situated.

SAFETY
Safe bikes
Make sure that your bike and those of any companions, especially children, are roadworthy. If you are not confident at cycle maintenance, get things checked before you go. Decide in advance what to do if your bike gets a puncture or breaks down.

Make sure you don't have things hanging off handlebars or panniers. Carrying things on your back is uncomfortable and the Highway Code prohibits the carrying of anything which will affect your balance. A purpose-made cycle bag is the only best means of carrying your belongings. Use your common sense about locking your bike but remember most insurance policies are void if you leave your bike unlocked. Remove valuables before leaving your bike.

Safe cycling
Wear comfortable clothes and shoes. Weather conditions change; allow storage for removed layers and carry spare clothes and appropriate waterproofs. Wearing a helmet will offer you some protection if you have an accident. Consider the regularity of refreshment stops, remember that in an ever-changing world you cannot rely on a single establishment being open, or even still being there. It is always wise to carry food and drink yourself. On a number of rides in this book it will be essential.

Stop if you want to consult a map or this book, otherwise you may ride into a car or a ditch. If you are with someone else or a group, make sure that the pace suits everyone.

If there is a chance that you will not return before dusk you will need to ensure that you have adequate front and rear lights and that your bike is fitted with a reflector.

Be prepared should something go wrong, but, above all, enjoy a safe trouble-free ride in glorious Devon.

ROUTE GRADINGS

Note: full routes are highlighted in bold type.

VERY EASY CIRCUITS
7   East Dartmoor villages and the Bovey valley *(5 mile section)*
8   The Haldon foothills and the Exe estuary *(7 mile section)*
11 East Devon excursion *(7 mile section)*
12 Culm Valley and Blackdown Hills *(11 mile section)*

EASY CIRCUITS
10 **The Otter valley** *(15 mile section or full 19 miles)*
13 Villages and hamlets of the Clyst valley *(16 mile section)*
14 Killerton estate, the Exe and tributary valleys *(either 13 mile section)*
19 Towards the source of the Tamar *(15 mile section)*

MODERATE CIRCUITS
1   **Lanes of the Denbury triangle** *(16 or 22 miles)*
2   Start Bay, Prawle Point and the Salcombe estuary *(7 mile section)*
4   **Moor to sea in the South Hams** *(22 or 26 miles)*
5   **The West Dartmoor foothills** *(15 or 23 miles)*
6   Dartmoor tors and legends *(10 or 15 mile sections)*
7   **East Dartmoor villages and the Bovey valley** *(12 miles)*
8   The Haldon foothills and the Exe estuary *(18 mile section)*
11 **East Devon excursion** *(26 miles)*
13 **Villages and hamlets of the Clyst valley** *(23 miles)*
14 **Killerton estate, the Exe and tributary valleys** *(25 miles)*
15 **The Grand Western Canal and the Lowman valley** *19 miles)*
16 **Mid Devon meander** *(20 miles)*
18 The Tarka Trail and the Yeo valley *(24 mile section)*
19 **Towards the source of the Tamar** *(23 miles)*

ADVENTUROUS CIRCUITS
2   **Start Bay, Prawle Point and the Salcombe estuary** *(24–27 miles)*
3   **The Avon valley and east Dartmoor foothills** *(16 or 18 miles)*
6   **Dartmoor tors and legends** *(25 miles)*
8   **The Haldon foothills and the Exe estuary** *(22 miles)*
9   **North-east Dartmoor** *(17 miles)*
12 **Culm Valley and Blackdown Hills** *(21 miles)*
17 **North-west corner** *(22, 27, or 35 miles)*
18 **The Tarka Trail and the Yeo valley** *(30 miles)*
20 **Okehampton and Dartmoor, Hatherleigh and Torridge** *(26 miles)*

Lanes of the Denbury triangle

16 or 22 miles

Bounded by the A38 expressway and the main roads linking Buckfastleigh, Totnes, Newton Abbot, and Bickington, there is a dense network of country lanes that pick their way between the rounded hills, and through the quiet valleys, farmsteads, and villages that typify this rural area. It is not an area of dramatic views, but it does offer very pleasant cycling along winding lanes in predominantly agricultural surroundings.

Map: OS Landranger 202 Torbay & South Dartmoor (GR 835665).

Starting point: This route starts by the church in Ipplepen. There is plenty of on-street parking in the village, or alternatively a short distance into the route is Orleigh Common, where there is a small car park. Ipplepen can be found off the A381 Totnes–Newton Abbot road. Follow the principal road through the village to the church, which is at the top of the main street.

Refreshments: There are two pubs and two shops in the village, and a café is located nearby in Fermoy's garden centre on the A381, about ¼ mile in the direction of Newton Abbot. Along the route there are pubs in Littlehempston, Woolston Green, Staverton, Broadhempston, Denbury, and East Ogwell, and there is a café just off the route at Landscove, in Hill House Nursery.

The route: This route does not include a main road; nor does it even cross one. Mostly it follows undulating, narrow country lanes which are rarely used by anything other than local traffic, and there is only one steep (but short) hill. With so many opportunities to stop along the way there is plenty of scope to recuperate if the ride is proving hard.

Public Transport: The nearest railway station is in Totnes. Follow the signs to Newton Abbot to join and follow the A381. The first left turn leads to Littlehemptston; join the route immediately after passing under the railway bridge.

---

1. Take Orleigh Road, past the recreation ground, west out of the village. Soon the road passes Orleigh Common on the left; the car park is on the right. After the descent **turn L** for Littlehempston (Pool Cross); the junction is located on a right-hand bend over the Am Brook stream. At the top of the rise is the small hamlet of Little

Steam train arriving at Staverton station

Ambrook and across the valley to the left is the odd form of the old monastic building of Great Ambrook.

Follow the lane until it ends at a crossroads (Fishacre Cross); here **turn L** to descend to and cross Am Brook at the double stone bridge. Immediately after this bridge, but before the railway bridge, **turn R** into a small lane. Follow this charming lane between the railway and the brook to Two Bridges; this is where the brook joins the River Hems. **Turn R** at the T-junction to cross both bridges and then **turn L** to follow the valley to Littlehempston.

2. **Turn R** at the T-junction past the Tally Ho Inn, which dates from the 14th century, and follow the long but gently meandering climb. Go **straight over** the first crossroads (Copper Tree Cross) At Waddons Cross there is the option of the longer or shorter route. (For the shorter route, **turn R** and follow the route from 5 below.)

3. Following a steady climb you are rewarded with fair views of Dartmoor in front and interrupted views through the hedgerows of the Dart Valley to your left. Keep straight on to a T-junction and here **turn R** to Landscove. The road soon descends to another T-junction, where again **turn R**, passing under power lines. Follow the road into Woolston Green, past

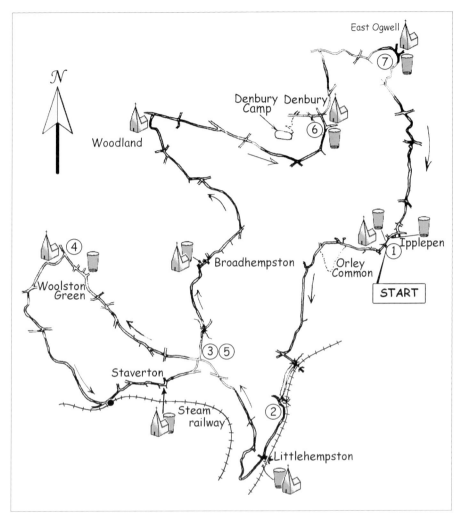

the Live and Let Live inn and a pretty green on your left.

4. Start climbing the hill towards the church and here **turn L**. Listen for the calls of the crows that inhabit the trees of the old vicarage, Hill House, which is now a plant nursery with pleasant tea rooms. Continue up the hill to reach the entrance. The route proceeds past Landscove's delightful little primary school and on into tiny lanes. At the T-junction **turn R**, for Ashburton, and then almost immediately **turn L** into a road signed as unsuitable for heavy vehicles. Cross the bridge over the river, looking out for the pretty garden to your left. Continue past the industrial sheds of Riverford Organic Vegetables on the right to the T-junction; **turn R** and climb sharply to another T-junction with a far wider road. **Turn L** and pass the National Grid Abham substation. The road drops to a pleasant shaded river, which is followed to a T-junction; **turn L** to Staverton Bridge station, where there is a collection of railway memorabilia. **Turn L** at the station in the direction of Staverton and follow the Dart Valley past the recreation ground to and through Staverton. Shortly after the Sea Trout inn, the road swings sharp left and climbs the steepest hill of the route; so get in the right gear. After a lane forking off to the right, the next crossroads is Waddons Cross (point 2 above).

5. Keep straight on and descend to the River Hems. Just after crossing the bridge, **turn L** and follow the river valley for about one mile, taking the first **turning R** (there is no signpost). Follow this lane into Broadhempston, passing the primary school before entering the village square, where you will find the church, the Monks Retreat pub, a children's play park, and the village store. **Turn R** at the T-junction in the square and then immediately **turn L**, signed to Denbury.

Ignore the road to the left signed to Woodland and Ashburton at The Old Smithy but keep straight on out of the village to the crossroads (Waterford Cross) and **turn L**. Climb the sharp rise to a ridge road.

Follow the lane, past a number of side roads, to and through the hamlet of Woodland. At the T-junction (Lane End), **turn R** for Denbury; follow the lane past many more side roads to the T-junction (Moorfoot Cross) and **turn R** for Denbury.

At the brow of the hill, ignore the left turn for Denbury and go straight on under the shadow of Denbury Clump. **Turn L** at the next crossroads by the dog kennels (Renwell Cross) for Denbury. This lane leads into the village at the green, which is overlooked by the Union Inn.

6. Proceed past the green to the T-junction in front of the great wall and **turn L** into the centre of the village. Ride to the square with the wall on your right, taking a peek at the Manor House through the arch. The junction at which three of the roads give way is marked by the war memorial.

(For a small excursion to Denbury Camp hillfort, turn left at the memorial and follow West Street to the edge of the village. The footpath leads up from opposite Denbury Down Lane, where there is a seat or road sign to which you could chain your bikes.)

Turn R at the memorial into East Street and pass Denbury prison on your right. Shortly after beginning the descent, take the **left fork** at Start Cross, for West Ogwell. On the junction is Denbury playing field, which includes a children's play area. It is well concealed from the road but is accessible through a gap in the hedge.

At the T-junction, **turn R;** look out for the fallen lime kiln at the summit of the small rise on your left. Cross **straight over** at the staggered crossroads (West Ogwell Cross) for East Ogwell. Climb the short sharp rise and follow the lane into East Ogwell.

7. Just after the road sweeps to the left as you descend into the village, **turn R** onto a minor road for Ipplepen; about 100 yards ahead is the Jolly Sailor pub. Follow the twisting lanes past various farms and a camp site, crossing **straight over** at the staggered crossroads at Rydon Cross and Dornafield Cross and finally at a second Dornafield Cross; all three are signed to Ipplepen.

The lane drops suddenly into Ipplepen and joins Bridge Street on a staggered crossroads. **Turn R** into the main lane through the village, passing the war memorial, the Wellington and the Plough pubs, and two convenience stores. The church, which marks the end of the route, is at the top of Bridge Street.

• •

SOUTH DEVON RAILWAY

The charming Staverton Station, with its original signal box, has appeared on television many times. It is situated halfway along the seven-mile Buckfastleigh to Totnes railway line, which is operated by the South Devon Railway Association. Steam trains are run regularly between mid-March and early November. At Buckfastleigh station is the Butterfly Farm and the Otter Sanctuary, whilst Totnes town centre is a short walk from Totnes station. When exploring the station, walk up to the bridge over the Dart, with its seven pointed arches and cutwaters, some containing seats. This is one of the oldest bridges in Devon, having been built in 1413.

DENBURY CAMP

This tree-capped rounded hill overlooking Teignbridge is now a principal landmark, and was once a strategically sited hillfort. It is believed that the fort was a defensive position of the Celtic Dumnonii against the invading Saxon forces. The fort itself has never been excavated and its date is unknown. It consists of two substantial round barrows contained within an elliptical ramparted area. The path to the fort is steep, but the views through the perimeter trees are extensive.

2

Start Bay, Prawle Point and the Salcombe estuary

7 or 24 to 27 miles

The drama and variety of the south-eastern corner of the South Hams is a delight to explore, and with so many lanes it is ideal for cycling. At one end of the ride is the Start Bay coastline, with the Slapton Ley Nature Reserve, and the famous ruined village of Hallsands. At the mid-point is the magnificent Salcombe estuary and the opportunity to take a short hop on a passenger ferry to see Salcombe itself. Secluded valleys, the charms of some typical South Hams villages, and even a paddle in the sea are there to be enjoyed en route.

Map: OS Landranger 202, Torbay & South Dartmoor (GR 824424).

Starting point: The car park is on the northern edge of the village of Torcross, adjacent to Slapton Ley on the A379. Parking charges apply seven days a week.

Refreshments: Cafés can be found in Torcross, South Hallsands, East Prawle, and East Portlemouth, with pubs in Torcross, Slapton, East Prawle, and just off-route in South Pool. There are also shops in Torcross and East Prawle.

The route: This is a generally undulating route with a few notable flat sections. Steep upward gradients are avoided, but there are a few long climbs and some steep descents. The route uses a popular tourist section of A-road at the start and finish and this road is also crossed once. Some sections of the lanes are also popular tourist routes. A number of the less well-used lanes are narrow, with varying qualities of surface finish. The route can be split in two; so that the Slapton and the Slapton Ley sections can be ridden as a separate ride from the Prawle peninsula and Salcombe estuary.

Public Transport: There is no railway station near the route.

1. **Turn L** out of the car park onto the gently curving A379 between the Ley and shore. Opposite the obelisk, **turn L** for Slapton and cross the bridge between the lower and higher Leys. Follow the road into Slapton village, **bearing R** past the Queens Arms. Pass under the steel bridge, noting the ruined tower which was part of a chantry dating from 1372.

2. Soon after the road starts climbing, **turn L** into the minor road just in front of the gable wall of Crossbow Cottage. At the T-

Slapton Ley from the Torcross viewpoint

junction **turn R** for the final climb out of the village. Cross **straight over** Townsend Cross for Chillaton and Stokenham and almost immediately **fork R** for Start. Following a short descent, **turn L** at the crossroads into a secluded valley. Follow the stream down the valley, past an old water wheel, and **turn R** at the T-junction and cross the stream, leaving it to flow on to feed the higher Ley. This is possibly the hardest hill of the ride. The line of trees marks the ramparts of an old earth fort though there is little of it to be seen now. The road passes through the ancient entrance to the fort and emerges in the level, protected heart; there is, however, a continuing rise from

the fort to a T-junction with a grass triangle (Colleridge Cross). **Turn L** for Stokenham and Torcross. Descend to a T-junction with a wider road and **turn R** to complete the descent to the roundabout on the A379.

3. Cross **straight over** for Prawle, East Portlemouth, and Beesands and follow the road over the hill. (On the right-hand bend is a turning, Mattiscombe Cross, to the left; for the shortcut follow this road back to the start.)

The descent that follows is fairly steep. **Turn L** at the bottom for Beeson and Beesands and immediately **fork R** into an

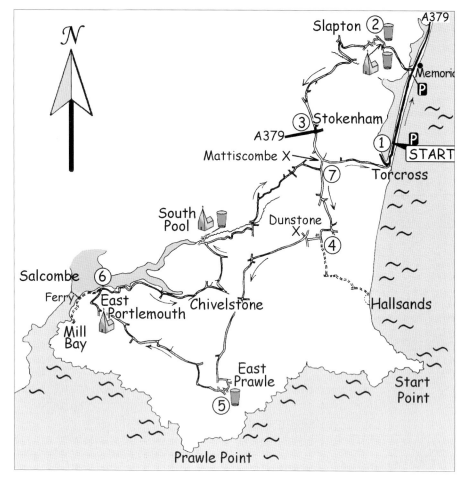

unsigned minor road. Follow this lane up the gentle rise, taking the first **turning R** at Huckam Barn Cross.

4. The lane soon descends past a few houses, look out for a **turning R** into an unsigned lane tucked in behind a former school playground; don't miss it!

Alternatively, to visit Hallsands keep straight on (this adds 2½ miles to the route). **Keep L** at two T-junctions to North Hallsands and then walk the coastal path, past the hotel to South Hallsands. Then retrace your route to point 4.

Climb from the former school to Dunstone Cross, and **turn R** at the T-junction and then immediately **turn L** at the crossroads. Follow the road until you, then pass the East Prawle village sign. Take the first **turning L**. Follow the road into a small dip, ignoring the left and right turns, and proceed to a T-junction; here **turn L** to emerge at the green, an ideal place for a rest.

5. With the green to the left, climb to the T-junction and **turn R** to follow the lane out of the village. Take the **first L turn**, which is located at the end of a long barn. At the next T-junction (Vinivers Cross), **turn L** for West Prawle and East Portlemouth. On entering East Portlemouth, note the steep gradient; there is a hairpin bend halfway down.

6. At the foot of the descent is a T-junction; **turn R** to join the tidal road which follows one of the creeks of the Salcombe Estuary.

Alternatively, **turn L** into a no through road, for an optional two mile, flatish excursion to Sandy Mill Bay beach, passing on your way an outdoor café, the ferry to Salcombe, and some public toilets. Return to the foot of the hill from East Portlemouth and head straight on along the tidal road.

Just after the ford, the road climbs steeply. Take the sharp **L turn** on the hill at Goodshelter Cross. This hill is a challenge, but thankfully it is short. Proceed over another gentle rise, past the end of the estuary, and dip down; just before the next ascent take a **R turn** at Devonshire Bridge for Chivelstone. About two thirds of the way up to the church take the really sharp **L**

turn back on yourself and continue to climb gently along the edge of the hillside to the apex, where there is a fabulous view across to Salcombe. Descend to the T-junction and **turn L** for South Pool. Just after the sharp bend on this descent, **turn sharp R** at Herring Street Cross for Ford. At the T-junction opposite Ford Farm, **turn L** to descend to the valley floor. Take the second **R turn** for Kernborough.

Take the first **R turn** (The Platt), for Kernborough. There follows a long and steady climb to Durlestone Cross; here cross **straight over** the staggered crossroads. Continue climbing, **keeping R** at the junction (which offers no indication of priorities). At the next T-junction, **turn L**.

7. Descend the left-hand bend and **turn R** (Mattiscombe Cross). Follow the lane to Torpoint; take care on the descent but do enjoy the views to your left of Slapton Ley by stopping at the Torcross viewpoint, which was formerly a private garden.

Keep **straight on** at the strange little crossroads by the car parking bays and then **turn R** at the T-junction to Slapton Ley. **Turn L** into the car park, but don't forget to enjoy a stroll on the magnificent shingle beach before you depart.

• •

HALLSANDS

It was during the period from 1897 to 1902 that dredgers removed the natural shingle bank that protected South Hallsands and transported the material to Plymouth Sound for the construction of a breakwater. The process that has provided protection for Plymouth ever since gradually led to the destruction of this once busy fishing village. Severe storm damage in 1903 and further coastal destruction meant that the village had to be abandoned in 1917.

SLAPTON AND THE LEY

Behind the three-mile beach is a naturally formed freshwater lake, known as the Ley. It is now a Site of Special Scientific Interest. On the small rise between the beach and the Ley is the longest level road in the South Hams. Mother Nature does her best to unite the Ley and sea in periodic storms, the most recent of which stripped a substantial length of the sandy soil away, including 100 yards of road.

In 1943 the occupants of much of the area were evacuated for secret army operations. The beach was used to practise for the D-Day landings. An obelisk stands approximately halfway along the beach, on the site of the Royal Sands Hotel, which did not survive the war. It was presented by the US army to those that left their homes and land. A more recent memorial is the Sherman tank which can be found in Slapton car park. It was retrieved from the sea in 1984 and serves as a memorial to the American servicemen who lost their lives when their amphibious landing craft was unexpectedly attacked by a German torpedo boat.

The Sherman tank at Slapton

The Avon valley and East Dartmoor foothills

16 or 18 miles

The River Avon rises on a part of Dartmoor known as Holne Moor. It soon flows into the resevoir contained by the Avon dam and then down through beautiful moorland scenery into a deep valley as it cascades its way to South Brent. From there it broadens out to meander along the flood plain, past Diptford, towards the sea. The route makes its way along these contrasting sections of the Avon upstream from Diptford and then climbs to the east into the foothills from where fine views can be enjoyed across Dartmoor and the South Hams.

Map: OS Landranger 202 Torbay & South Dartmoor (GR 697603).

Starting point: The public car park beside the railway line in South Brent, off the B3372, just to the north of the A38. Turn into the village from the roundabout and carry straight on past the church, turning into the car park just before the railway bridge.

Refreshments: There are shops and pubs in South Brent. Rattery and Avonwick also have pubs, but there are no cafés on the route.

The route: The eastern foothills of Dartmoor are quite hilly, and, whilst this route threads its way through the easier roads, it is generally undulating and there are some steeper climbs. The route has four crossings of busy roads, one of which involves following a well-used downgraded B-road for a quarter of a mile. Otherwise the lanes are narrow, with loose surfaces in places. Shipley Bridge is a popular tourist attraction; the road to Bloody Pool Cross is consequently busier than might otherwise be expected for a narrow lane. The ride can be shortened by turning before Diptford for South Brent; this also avoids a hill.

Public Transport: The nearest railway station is on the main line at Ivybridge, some four miles from the start. Turn left from the station and under the railway viaduct at Bittaford to climb steeply up a lane that leads to South Brent.

---

1. Ride away from the car park with the railway line on your right. At the T-junction **turn R** and immediately cross the railway line and **turn L** at the T-junction. Pass the country house to your left and then drop down to the first crossing of the River Avon at the rather picturesque Lydia Bridge.

The author cycling away from Shipley Bridge

It is here that hard effort is needed to assail the hardest hill of the ride. On the right near the top is Penstave Copse, owned by the Woodland Trust. You are welcome to enter; so why not recuperate whilst enjoying the open views through the sapling trees. Drop back down to ride alongside the Avon and work your way upstream to Shipley Bridge.

2. This is the next crossing point of the Avon; it is also the site of a large car park and toilets are available here.

Beside the bridge is a tarmac bridlepath to the Avon Dam, which makes an ideal and well-graded cycle route right onto the moor two miles distant. It is a popular route for walkers and families and cycles should therefore be used with extra care.

Cross the bridge and continue along the route, across a ford, and up a gentle climb. On the following descent, you face the gentle grassy slope of Brent Hill; the scarp slope is completely out of view for now. A tougher climb follows to Bloody Pool Cross; **turn L** here for Gidley and Skerraton.

The road soon descends sharply to Gidley Bridge, after a short rise **turn R** at the unsigned T-junction. Shortly **fork R** into a side road for Dean and Buckfastleigh. Go straight over at the crossroads and at the T-junction **turn R**, going back on yourself (Clampitts Cross); there is no sign. At the crossroads (Dean Cross), **turn L** for Rattery and climb over a small hill to the crossing of the A38. Then take the first left after the dual carriageway slip road for Smallacombe, Pennywell, and Bigadon. At the crossroads (Smallcombe Cross) continue **straight over** for Pennywell and Bigadon.

3. At the T-junction pause to enjoy the wide views that extend from Dean Moor, past Buckland Beacon, towards Haytor, and then round towards Torquay. **Turn R** here; there is no signpost.

Follow the narrow lane past a few side turnings and continue down a long shallow descent to Rattery. **Turn R** at the T-junction (Almhouse Cross) for Rattery and South Brent and pass the village sign. Descend steeply into the

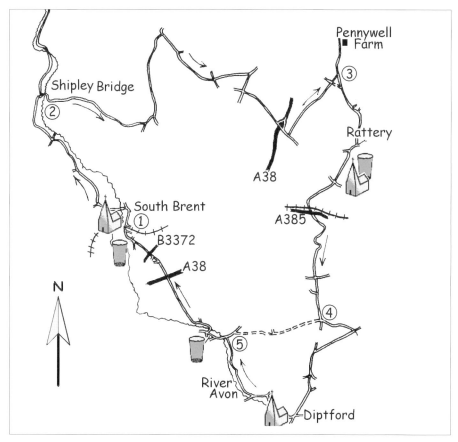

village and then climb up, passing the pub and the church. Continue straight on at the crossroads at the brow of the hill and descend to and under the main line railway viaduct to reach the A385. Take care crossing the main road: the visibility is not good. There is no signpost. After crossing the brook there follows a short pull. Proceed upwards to the crossroads (Shorter Cross) with the downgraded B-road. Cross **straight over** for Diptford and Morleigh

4. Just before the road climbs again, **turn left** at the crossroads (Kerswell Cross). (There is no signpost.)

(To take the **shortcut** to Avonwick, **turn R** here for Elwell and follow the road to the T-junction by Charford Chapel conversion; here **turn L** onto the main road into Avonwick (point 5).)

Proceed with care along the narrow and bumpy lane, past Kerswill Farm and on to the T-junction;

here **turn R** (there is no signpost). Climb up alongside the Lincombe valley; this is a long gentle drag to an unsigned T-junction on the ridge; **turn L** and cross the head of the valley.

Take the first **fork R** at a grass triangle into a minor road (Diptford Green) for Diptford. Descend round a few twists, passing Diptford Court Farm on the right and heading into the village of Diptford. Follow the road round to the right, passing the school and the church on the left. Proceed down a most enjoyable twisting descent to the Avon river, arriving in the flood plain near the cricket pitch. Follow the river and the course of the old railway line.

5. A sharp incline brings an abrupt end to the blissfully quiet and level road. At the T-junction (Avonwick Bridge), **turn L** for Avonwick and South Brent. Drop down over the railway and river bridges into Avonwick and past the Avon Inn. Look out for a small crossroads at the end of the village (Old Bridge) and **turn R** here for Horsebrook. Cross the Avon again on a steep humpback bridge and then climb steadily to cross the A38. Descend to the roundabout on the B3372 and cross **straight over** into Totnes Road. (It is signed for the village centre and there is a play area and shelter on the right.)

Turn **R** at the T-junction in the centre of South Brent and follow

the road into a one-way street. Continue past the church and on to the railway bridge. **Turn R** into the side road immediately before the bridge to get to the car park.

• •

AVON DAM
High and deep into the South Moor is the Avon reservoir. I find the route to it from Shipley Bridge a greater delight than the reservoir itself. Starting in the lush valley, the traffic-free road climbs at an easy gradient with the river Avon rushing in its ravine alongside. To the left, just before the road leaves the woodland, are the remains of Brentmoor House, which was once at the heart of a 3,000 acre estate. As you thread your way through the rolling Dartmoor hills, the flow of the stream reduces. But then listen out for the sound of the great white wall that emerges around the last bend. This is the overflow of the dam and can be quite beautiful and yet terrifying when up close.

SOUTH BRENT
The village of South Brent nestles under the shadow of Dartmoor, in particular Brent Hill and the majestic Ugborough Beacon. The village has a great reputation for its night-time carnival and its amateur dramatics group. It is a busy place, with some useful shops where you can stock up with provisions for a day's ride. Look out for the old tollhouse and the list of charges that were made on market days.

There is a strange tale to tell of an incident in 1436 in St Petroc's church. A blocked-up doorway can be seen in the north-west corner, and it is through this door that for some unknown reason the parson was dragged from evensong and then beaten to death.

Moor to sea in the South Hams

22 to 26 miles

From the old mill town of Ivybridge, this route follows the ridge roads between the rivers Erme and Yealm until the landmass cascades into the English Channel. At the start the Erme is a youthful river, fresh with clear dancing water, having just descended from the wet moorland of south Dartmoor. At the halfway point is the gorge-like estuary of the Yealm, as it breaks out through the dramatic cliffs. There is variety in abundance in what is designated an Area of Outstanding Natural Beauty.

Map: OS Landranger 202 Torbay & South Dartmoor (GR 636561).

Starting point: The leisure centre car park in the centre of Ivybridge. The entrance can be found off a roundabout next to the police station and is well signed. It is a pay-and-display car park that is free on Sundays, but please check for changes.

Refreshments: There is a café in the leisure centre and one in the adjacent arcade, as well as many food outlets and pubs in Ivybridge. Along the way are pubs in Noss Mayo and Ermington. In addition, there is a café in Endsleigh Garden Centre and two pubs just off the route in Holbeton.

The route: Most of the route is on lanes, some of which are narrow. There is a short section of busier road in the first mile, a well-used downgraded B-road at the finish, and half a mile downhill on an A-road that can be busy at commuting times and in holiday periods. The clifftop road towards Noss Mayo can be busy at times with leisure traffic drawn by the popular coastal walks. There are two large climbs, the first fairly steep and right at the start, the second more gentle but prolonged after Noss Mayo.

Public Transport: There is a railway station in Ivybridge. Turn right out of the station and follow the directions for through traffic until you reach the leisure centre roundabout.

1. Follow the one-way system through the car park and cross **straight over** the roundabout into Woolcombe Lane. Take the first **R turn** into Paddock Drive, following the Plymouth cycle path signs. At the end of Paddock Drive, ride over the dropped kerb and through the bollards to a Transco gas meter housing and here **turn L** to follow the narrow path alongside a grassy strip by the River Erme. **Fork R** and

23

Eastern Lodge on the Membland Estate

go through the A38 underpass (watch for broken glass outside the recycling centre).

At the main road **turn R**, signed to Ivybridge and Endsleigh Garden Centre. You will soon pass a sign stating that you are entering Ivybridge; do not be concerned. Shortly the road rises to a T-junction, where you **turn L**, taking care, as this is the A38 slip road. Just before the end of the slip road, **turn L** towards the Endsleigh Garden Centre. Continue along the lane up a large hill.

The summit is Todd Moor, a nature reserve of wet heathy grassland. Look out for the interesting

population of birdlife here, and then descend into Westlake.

On the left-hand bend in the village (Westlake Cross) **turn R**, and then immediately **turn L** (Russetts Cross), both are signed to Burraton and Yealmpton. These rural lanes with their high hedgerows are typical of the South Hams. You will soon reach a **L turn** (Luson Cross) opposite a farm. There is no signpost; so make sure you don't miss it.

Follow the lane over a hill, after a while **fork L**; the junction is unmarked, and is again easily missed. Soon you will emerge from the tiny lanes onto the A379 at a crossroads. Cross **straight over** for Holbeton, Mothecombe, Batisborough, and Alston. Take care as this road can be very busy.

2. There follows a gentle drag, but the reward is more than worth the effort. The top is marked by the imposing Bull and Bear Lodge that once served the old Membland estate.

Continue along the lane. Before long you will pass Eastern Lodge, a charming gatehouse which marked another of the drives to Membland House. On the sharp right bend (Stoke Cross), take the **second left**, which is effectively straight on, for Netton and Worswell. Soon you pass a turning for a National Trust car park where the end of the coastal carriage drive can be reached.

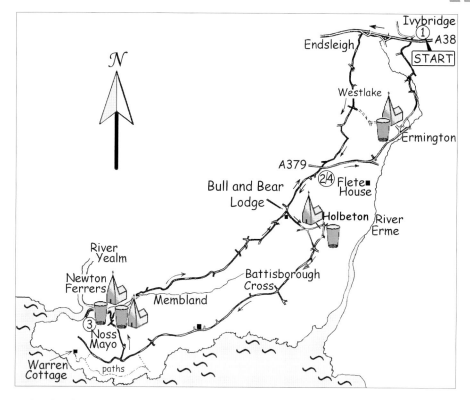

Take the first **turning R** (Langdon Hill Cross) for Noss Mayo.

(To complete the ridge ride continue straight on to Worswell. After a small climb, pass another National Trust car park, quite close to Warren Cottage. After one mile the road runs out at Worswell Farm, but stop at the double bend and enjoy the fantastic panoramic views. Return to Langdon Hill Cross.)

Take the **first L**, which can be found before crossing the stream. Follow the valley down to Noss Mayo, **turning L** at the first T-junction and **right** at the second.

(Another short detour is highly recommended here. Instead of turning right into Friary Hill, keep straight on alongside the estuary on Passage Road. Shortly after passing the Newton Ferrers ferry you will catch a view down the estuary and to Plymouth Sound at the Kilpatric Steps. This marks the end of the road but descend the steps and enjoy the well-positioned seats. Return to Friary Hill Road.)

3. Climb the sharp hill past the Swan Inn. At the summit is a T-junction (Junket Cross); **turn L** and return to river level, crossing the estuary by an unexpectedly small bridge at Bridgend. **Turn R** here

25

into the second road on the right, for Preston. As the road starts to climb take the first **R turn** (Clanicombe Cross), for Preston. This is the start of the long rise out of the Yealm Valley; so settle into an easy gear and enjoy the views. Ignore the right turn for Preston and keep straight on at Darkey Hill. Finally the hill is conquered and before you, across the fields, is Dartmoor. A relaxing pedal on peaceful level roads leads you to a T-junction (Creacombe Cross); **turn R** for Holbeton. Soon after, at the next T-junction (Bull & Bear Cross), **turn L** to retrace the outward route to the A379.

4. Turn R onto the A379 and continue for a mile, predominantly downhill. Look out for Flete House across the valley to your right. (If the road is busy you can return via Westlake, turning right in the village and following the signs to Ermington.)

Take the **L fork** on to the A3121, signed to Ugborough, and **fork L** into Town Hill at the old toll house. A small rise brings you into the market square of Ermington.

Keep right out of the square. Follow the Erme valley road towards Ivybridge. After crossing the river, ignore the first right, to Penquit, but take the next **turn R** on a left-hand bend into a minor road. There is no signpost. Pass under the

A38 and then immediately **turn L** (Woolcombe Lane – unsigned) into a housing estate and continue to a roundabout, where you go **straight over** into the leisure centre.

• •

ERMINGTON AND FLETE

There is a charm about Ermington. From the sloping town square cast your eye upon the church spire and you will note that it is twisted in a similar manner to the more famous Chesterfield spire. At the church you will see the monumental lychgate with its grandiose flights of steps, stone arches and heavy columns. Much of the church was refitted for Henry Mildmay of Flete, whose home can be found less than two miles downstream in the Erme valley. The castellated house gained its present romantic form at the hands of the architect Norman Shaw after Mildmay had purchased it in 1878.

MEMBLAND HOUSE AND THE CARRIAGE DRIVE

The banker Edward Baring, who became Lord Revelstoke, transformed the house during the time it was in his ownership between 1877 and 1916. The house was located in the valley to the east of Noss Mayo, and its influence can be seen around the area. The many lodges on the estate were built in the same romantic style with deep bracketed eaves. Membland was sold when Barings went through a financial crisis; by 1939 the house was in ruins and it was demolished at the end of the war.

From the house is the 10 mile carriage drive. First it follows the estuary through Noss Mayo and then along the cliff edge known as the Warren to Stoke Point, from where the drive returns to Membland.

The West Dartmoor foothills

15 or 23 miles

Between the Tamar river and the massive granite uplands of Dartmoor lies the Tavy river. The scenery that borders this tributary of the Tamar is both dramatic and beautiful. There is plenty of low-lying moorland, as well as some pleasant villages and the ancient stannary town of Tavistock which are well worth exploring. The route is sufficiently elevated to offer extended views across east Cornwall and west Devon. The most remarkable views of all, however, are to be seen from Brent Tor, a must on a clear day. There are also a number of tors and the delightful Tavy Cleave that are easily accessible from the route.

Map: OS Landranger 201 Plymouth & Launceston (GR 480744).

Starting point: The Meadowlands pay-and-display car park in Bedford Street, Tavistock.

Refreshments: Refreshments are available at the Meadowlands indoor swimming pool or in the adjacent town. Along the way are pubs in Peter Tavy, Horndon, Mary Tavy, and near Brent Tor. There are no cafés on the route.

The route: With the exception of a short distance of main road in Tavistock, the route follows minor roads, occasionally crossing a main road. The lanes are narrow with variable surfaces. A cycle route on an old railway track is used for the return into Tavistock. Although steep hills are largely avoided, this is generally rolling countryside, with an ascending tendency for the first half of the ride. Be aware that some sections are poorly signed. The distance of this route can be reduced by following the A386 back to Tavistock from Mary Tavy.

Public Transport: The nearest railway station is in Bere Alston, some six miles away. Climb through the village from the station and follow the B3257 for Tavistock, turning right after crossing the valley for Crowndale. Bus route 86 between Plymouth and Barnstaple stops at Tavistock. Operated by First, it carries bikes.

---

1. **Turn R** out of the car park, over the pedestrian crossing, past the Bedford Hotel, and on towards the pannier market. **Turn R** at the roundabout, cross over the pelican crossing and river bridge, and then at the next roundabout, **turn R** for Whitchurch. The road climbs gently to a wide junction on the brow of the hill; **turn L** here for Whitchurch Down. It may be called Down Road, but it certainly does not go down; instead it climbs to the moor; a cattle grid marks

The church at Brent Tor

your arrival. Wind your way around the golf clubhouse and first tee to reach the open moor.

Follow the road past a few junctions to Moortown Cross, where you **turn L** for Moortown. Pew Tor towers above to the right. As the road turns to descend, on the sky line in front is a pointed hill on which stands Brent Tor church; this will be visited later on the route. Descend to a stream (here the road edge is bounded by stone bollards in lieu of a wall). Soon after starting up the climb, **turn R** into a straight level road to a T-junction; **turn R** for Princetown and descend to a river bridge.

Proceed over the bridge and up a slight pull to the main road at Moorshop. Cross **straight over** for Peter Tavy and on to Route 27. Just before the road descends steeply, **turn R** for Sowton Town, staying on Route 27. Shortly after Sowton Farm, **turn L** at the T-junction (right is a dead end). Almost immediately, **turn L** at a grass triangle and continue descending to **turn R** at the next two T-junctions. You know that you have got through this maze of lanes correctly if you find yourself heading towards the grand church tower that announces your arrival at Peter Tavy.

2. Climb to and through the village. Just before the dead end sign, **turn L** for Willsworthy and Hilltown, and drop to Hill Bridge, a crossing point of the Tavy. Take the inevitable climb up the opposite hillside. At the top look up to the tors and you may see the red flag flying for the Willsworthy firing range, which occupies much of this corner of Dartmoor. Shortly take the **L fork** for Horndown and Mary Tavy to complete the climb, and

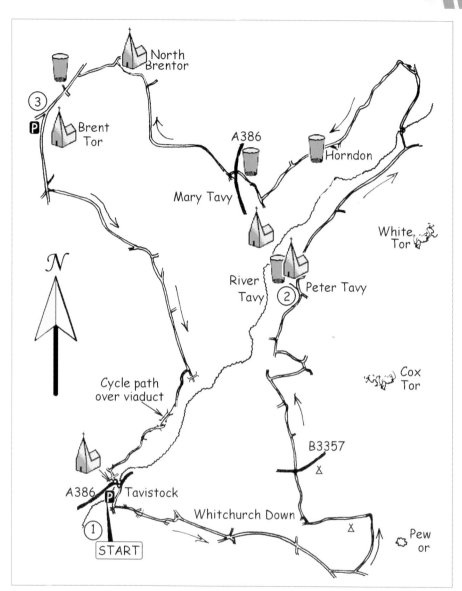

thus to turn away from Tavy Cleave and the high moor. There are better views than ever to be savoured now.

(To visit Tavy Cleave, turn right at the previous fork and climb to the car park a mile along the lane. Park your bike and follow the track to the right for about a mile to reach the Cleave.)

After a long run down, **turn R** at the T-junction for Tavistock and

29

Okehampton, which is more or less opposite Mary Tavy school. After the dip, climb up to the A386 by the war memorial and cross **straight over** into Chapel Lane alongside the Methodist chapel. **Turn R** at the crossroads for some gentle climbs across some really magnificent moorland towards the humble church that sits on the imposing Brent Tor.

Drop down over the river bridge and then climb into North Brentor. **Turn L** at the T-junction by the war memorial. Follow the road round to the right and up out of the village to a T-junction, where you **turn L** for Tavistock to climb to Brent Tor. This road carries a larger volume of traffic.

3 To visit the church, fork right on the brow of the hill for the car park; otherwise keep straight on for Tavistock. Toilets are available here.

On the way down the hill there are two left turns very close to each other: take the **second L**, which is again signed Route 27. Eventually the gradient increases, but look out for the old railway viaduct and **turn R** into narrow lane about a 100 yards before it, thus remaining on Route 27.

Just before the steep descent, **turn R** into an opening marked by a granite boulder and onto a short section of railway track, which almost immediately crosses a wide viaduct. Then rejoin the road, **turning L**, and descend past the next opening on to the railway track and into Tavistock town centre. **Turn L** at the T-junction. Look up to the right to see the great viaduct. Cross **straight over** the first roundabout and **turn R** at the next roundabout.

The car park can be found on the **left** just after the second pedestrian crossing.

● ●

MARY, PETER, AND THE TAVY
On opposite banks of the Tavy river are the two villages of Mary Tavy and Peter Tavy. Each has a church, not surprisingly named St Mary's and St Peter's, respectively. The villages were home to workers in the copper, arsenic, lead, and silver mines, the ruins of which can be seen around the area, together with the numerous leats that were required to operate the machinery. At one time Wheal Friendship in Mary Tavy was the largest copper mine in the world.

BRENT TOR
A highly visible landmark on the western edge of Dartmoor is the church of St Michael de la Rupe (of the rock) on Brent Tor. It was built by Robert Giffard, the lord of the manor of Lamerton, and dates from about 1130. However, legend has it that a wealthy merchant, caught in a terrible storm, promised the Almighty that if he survived he would build a church on a prominent landmark. Arriving in Devonport, he spotted Brent Tor to the north and made his way there to build this church. It is a steep walk up to the church, but the views in every direction are spectacular.

Dartmoor tors and legends

10, 15, or 25 miles

Dartmoor is an awe-inspiring landscape with its majestic hills and craggy tors. Add to this the quaint villages, the archaeological remains, and the grazing animals at the side of open moorland roads and it all adds up to a wonderful place in which to cycle. There are some notes of caution that should be heeded when cycling in remote areas such as Dartmoor: the high moor suffers extreme and rapidly changing weather conditions; there are not many shops or even houses so self-sufficiency is important. Be prepared, and you will enjoy the immense diversity of this route, on which there is so much to see.

Map: OS Landranger 191 Okehampton & North Dartmoor (GR 719768).

Starting point: The public car park in Widecombe. The village is to be found six miles west of Bovey Tracey on the B3387, which in turn is signed off the A38 at Drum Bridges.

Refreshments: In addition to the eating places in Widecombe, there is a very popular refreshments van at Houndtor, which is open at weekends all year, and on weekdays in summertime. There is also a pub in Manaton.

The route: The route contains two loops, thus allowing for the ride to be truncated or enjoyed in two halves. The steepest hills are descended on the ride. Of course, this does mean that there are some long climbs, although the route is generally rolling in nature and, apart from two short stretches on B-roads, it follows minor roads, which can be quite busy as they are in a popular part of the national park.

Public Transport: The nearest railway station is in Newton Abbot. It is a long ride, with substantial climbing, and so is impractical for all but stronger cyclists.

1. Turn R out of the car park and pass the green to the right and church to the left for Buckland in the Moor, Dartmeet, and Postbridge. Soon the village is behind you, although it is worth pausing to look back from the apex of the gentle rise at the grandeur of the church tower nestling under the dramatic Dartmoor hills. (Ignore the first right turn; this is a shortcut but involves one of the hardest climbs on Dartmoor.) After approximately one mile on the generally climbing hedged lane, take the next **R turn**, shortly before the warning signs for the narrow bridge (Easton Lane Cross), for

At the summit of the climb past Grimspound

Postbridge, Princetown, and Moretonhampstead. The climbing now gets a little steeper, but at the summit is the reward of arriving on the open moor. Follow this lane into and up the valley with Hamel Down to your right and Challacombe Down to your left.

The moorland farmsteads give way to open grazing as the road works its way up the valley. Just after the hairpin bend is a layby and opposite is a path that leads onto the moor to Grimspound. It is not signed but is easy to find. The views at the summit are worth savouring.

2. Descend to the T-junction (Challacombe Cross) with the B3212, one of the two main roads that cross Dartmoor, and **turn R** for Moretonhampstead. On the left is a popular viewing point. The descent continues, steeper now – watch the left-hand bend as it gets sharper as you continue. Then cross the cattle grid and continue on the main road. **Turn R** at the first road on the right, which is after about half a mile (Watching Place); this is a minor road for Manaton. Presiding over the junction is an old stone cross. The road is known as 'Long Lane', perhaps from the days when it was a B-road full of larger vehicles. You are now heading along the eastern side of Hamel Down.

3. After approximately two miles is a crossroads (Heatree Cross). (For the shortcut option **turn R** through

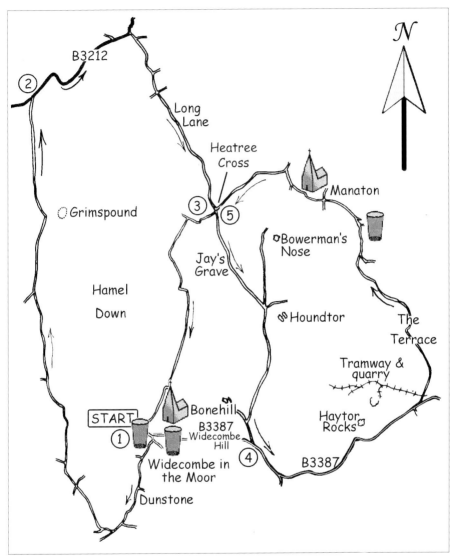

the stone gate posts and follow the final section of this route from point 5.)

Continue straight on for Houndtor, Haytor, and Widecombe, climbing up onto the most beautiful of the open moorland that Dartmoor can

offer for cyclists. The route continues on the same road past Jays Grave and Houndtor, drops into a little dip, after which Bone Hill Rocks can be seen to the right.

4. Continue to a T-junction (Hareford Cross) and **turn L** onto the B3387, signed Haytor and Bovey Tracey (right takes you straight down the infamous 1:5 Widecombe Hill to the village). Ride across the head of the valley that becomes the Leighton estate leading on down to Manaton. Enjoy the descent of Haytor Hill, taking the **first turning L**. This lane to Manaton hugs the hillside and has great views across Trendlebere Down and the Bovey basin. First the road climbs past the Haytor Granite Tramway (see route 7). The descent at the end of the lane is steep and slippery, and at the bottom is a hump back bridge on a sharp bend.

At the T-junction (Leighton Cross), **turn L** past the Kestor Inn, and on past Manaton with its pretty green; eventually you will reach Heatree Cross (3 above).

5. Cross **straight over** for Heathercombe and Natsworthy and up to the top of the ridge. At the brow of the hill **turn L** and follow the ridge, with Hammerdown on your right.

The return to Widecombe consists of a fine descent in narrow twisting lanes down the Natsworthy valley.

● ●

HAYTOR

Perhaps the most famous of the tors is Haytor rocks. In Victorian times charabanc rides would visit from the coastal resort of Torbay. At this time steps were carved into the rock to allow the visiting parties to reach the top. The old iron handrail has corroded away but the highly polished steps remain. They take a little finding but are located roughly in the middle of the elevation overlooking Haytor Hill and the lowlands beyond. The steps start about three yards up the rocks, and there are sections that you need to climb and jump as the steps have some gaps, but the view!

GRIMSPOUND

To the western edge of the parish of Manaton is the Bronze Age enclosure of Grimspound. A short walk from the road alongside a babbling brook brings you to the pound wall. This wall, once 1.6 yards high, 3 yards wide and 500 yards in circumference encloses 4 acres of land, in which are the circular outlines of 24 huts. Such circles are commonly found on Dartmoor, but not in such large groups. The history of the pound is uncertain.

JAY'S GRAVE

In a gateway on what was once a crossroads on an ancient route is a grave. On that grave are flowers, always fresh. Nobody, they say, changes the flowers; they are just always there. The grave, known as Jay's Grave, is that of Kitty Jay. Hers is a sad story. She was a servant girl at Canna Farm, who became pregnant and was so ashamed that she hung herself in a barn. Church law at the time ruled that those who committed suicide could not be buried in consecrated ground, but instead at a crossroads so that the troubled souls would not find their way back.

East Dartmoor villages and the Bovey valley

5 or 12 miles

The Bovey basin is renowned for its ball clay, and much of the old flood plains of the rivers Bovey and Teign has been excavated to extract this rich deposit. The route skirts along the edge of the Bovey basin, benefiting from the level roads but mercifully distant from the opencast clay mining. Turning in to the foothills of Dartmoor, the route passes remains of the Granite Tramway as well as the nature reserve of Yarner Wood on its way to the picture postcard village of Lustleigh, one of the most delightful villages in the national park. The return route passes the country estate of Parke, with its woodland and riverside walks.

Map: OS Landranger 191 Okehampton & North Dartmoor (GR 814783).

Starting point: The public car park by the river in Bovey Tracey. The town is signed from the A38 dual carriageway at Drum Bridges. Follow the signs for the town centre; the car park is on the right just before the river crossing. Toilets and tourist information are located in the car park.

Refreshments: There are numerous cafés in Bovey Tracey, and one in Lustleigh. Pubs can be found in Bovey Tracey, near Cummings Cross, and in Lustleigh.

The route: The route contains two loops, thus allowing for the ride to be truncated. The first loop, which is ideal for beginners, has very gentle rolling hills and is in country lanes after leaving Bovey. The second loop is rather hillier; the lanes are narrower with poor surfaces in some sections; and there is one steep descent. The last section includes ½ mile of narrow A-road, although an old railway line can be followed to avoid the A-road.

Public Transport: The nearest railway station is in Newton Abbot. There is a signed cycle route from Newton Abbot to Bovey Tracey; it joins this route at point 2, which is approximately six miles from the station.

---

1. **Turn L** out of the car park and **turn L** into Newton Road, just after the Brookside Tea Rooms. Immediately before the parish church of St John the Evangelist **turn R** into Ashburton Road. Cross **straight over** at the crossroads (Thorn's Cross) to continue on Ashburton Road. Take care on this small descent, as there is a

Bovey Tracey Mill, now the Devon Guild of Craftsmen

narrowing of the road. Where the road width returns look to the left to see Blue Waters Lake, the remains of a former clay working. This road, which forms the national park boundary, dips down and up twice, the second time alongside forestry land known as the Great Plantation, which is accessible on foot from either of two locations.

2. Go **straight over** at the next crossroads (Cummings Cross) and drop down to a stream on the left with a row of cottages on the right. Immediately after the cottages, **turn R** into a small lane for Rora. Continue to the end of the lane

and cross **straight over** the staggered crossroads on the edge of Liverton. Follow the lane all the way to Brimley.

3. At the crossroads (Brimley Cross), **turn L** for Higher Brimley and Ilsington and then almost immediately **turn L** again at the next T-junction.

(It is from here that you can **turn R** to return to Bovey Tracey, **turning L** at the T-junction opposite Brimley Post Office and thus joining the outward route.)

Upon reaching the end of the housing, **turn R** (Chapple Cross) into Chapple Road for Haytor and Manaton and follow the national park boundary again. Drop to a left- and then a right-hand bend and look out for the sign for the Templer Way. Beneath the sign are the carved stones of the old stone tramway. As you ride on, you see further remains of the tramway in the grass verge to your left, until, at the next right bend, it goes into the woods to start its long steady ascent to Haytor.

Climb up the short haul to the B3387 (Lowerdown Cross) and cross **straight over** at the Edgemoor Hotel for Lowerdown, Becky Falls, and Manaton. The upward pull continues past some pleasant country homes and to the cries of birdlife on this wooded hilltop. Drop to the T-junction (Gypsy Corner) and **turn L** for

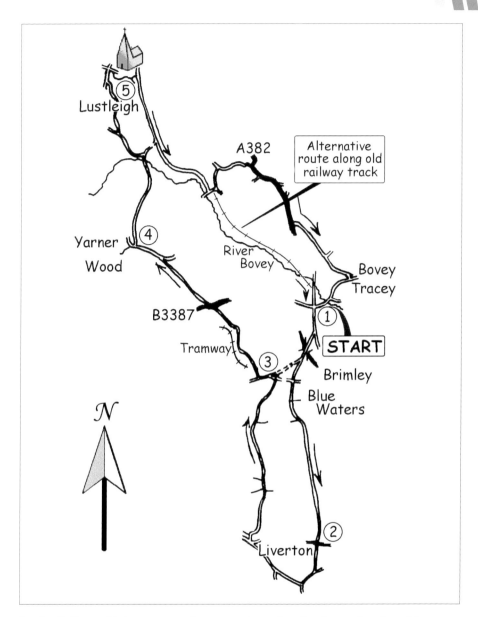

Becky Falls and Manaton and into the Dartmoor National Park.

4. At the bottom of the dip (Reddaford Water), **turn R** into the minor road for Lustleigh. On the junction look out for the old boundary stone tucked under the rhododendron bushes.

(To visit Yarner Wood continue up the B road towards Lustleigh for about 300 yards and **turn L** into the level drive where the main road swings sharply to the right.)

Climb up through the woods and then down steeply to the river Bovey, which is crossed on an old stone bridge. Soon after **turn L** into a small side road for Rudge and Sanduck. As the road swings to the right it climbs sharply up the hardest climb of the ride. **Turn R** into the first road to the right, which is not signed. The narrow and gravelly road eventually drops to a delightful river valley which leads into Lustleigh.

At the T-junction, **turn R** for Moretonhampstead and immediately cross the bridge into the village. Turn right at the crossroads, under the shadow of the church tower, for Bovey Tracey and Moretonhampstead. The play park is to your left (signed 'toilets') at this junction.

5. **Turn R** down the slope between Primrose Cottage and the memorial. Walk the bike through the narrow pathway, across the stone bridge over the leat, and round the sharp bends under the railway bridge. Remount to ride along this very narrow lane past the cricket pitch and on through the breathtaking hamlet of Wreyland. Follow the road round to the **left** at Wreyland Manor and climb up to the T-junction and **turn R**.

Having left the views of Lustleigh

behind, descend to the sharp right-hand bend and here **turn L** for Bovey Tracey, which is effectively straight on. Drop down under the railway bridge and alongside the river Bovey under the dappled shade of the riverside woodland. Follow it to the T-junction (Willford Bridge) and **turn L** for Moretonhampstead and Bovey Tracey.

Ride between the piers of the old railway bridge to the T-junction.

(From here you can **turn R** between the railway pier and the junction through a gate and follow a path onto the bed of the old railway line. You then follow this back to Bovey Tracey, if you wish. However, it can be muddy in parts and you may prefer to stay on the road – if so, follow the directions below.)

Turn L at this grass triangle and follow the valley to an unsigned T-junction. **Turn R** and climb up this narrow lane complete with its central line of mossy grass to the main road. **Turn R** at the T-junction (Kings Cross) onto the A382 for Bovey Tracey. After passing the sign for Bovey Tracey the road opens out. **Turn L** at the wide junction into Moretonhampstead Road, signed to the hospital. Follow the road through the northern edge of Bovey until the road swings sharply down to the right to a T-junction by the town hall. **Turn R** into High Street and descend through the shopping centre to the river bridge; soon after the car park is to be found on the left.

Wreyland Manor near Lustleigh

BOVEY TRACEY

The area around the town is rich in clay deposits and an active pottery industry developed to the south-east of Bovey Tracey. Remains of it can be seen at the House of Marbles, now better known for glass blowing, wooden toys, and marbles; the marble runs are a sight to behold. Maintaining the pottery tradition is Cardew, albeit with a modern approach to their teapots. In the old mill in the centre of the town is the Devon Guild of Craftsmen, which maintains a permanent display of work from craftsmen across Devon and has regular craft-related exhibitions. The Bovey Handloom Weavers offers the opportunity to learn about the weaving process.

HAYTOR GRANITE TRAMWAY

It was in 1820 that the parallel granite rails running from Haytor to Stover were opened. The principle was simple, the ballast – namely, the granite that had been quarried – was loaded onto small trucks, 13 ft long. Gravity carried these trucks all the way to Stover and from there a canal carried the cargo to the river Teign, at the mouth of which was Teignmouth Docks. The empty trucks were then pulled back to the quarries by carthorses. On the seven-mile outward journey, a brave soul would sit on the trucks operating a 10-foot pole levered against a wheel to serve as a brake as it dropped the 1,300 ft to Stover. It fell into disuse in 1858, having been replaced by new modes of transport.

YARNER WOOD

Yarner Wood is a National Nature Reserve, owned by English Nature. On either of the two nature trails ash, alder, birch, beech, rowan, sycamore, and pine can be found alongside both native species of oak. Along the trails you can see the granite tramway and the remains of a copper mine that once employed 50 men. A warden's office and visitor centre has recently been constructed, achieving minimal environmental impact with its sustainable concept.

The Haldon foothills and the Exe estuary

7, 18, or 22 miles

Sandwiched between the Haldon ridge and the Exe estuary is a fine selection of country lanes that meander through rich agricultural land, interspersed with charming hamlets and roadside thatched cottages. The coastal section of the route passes a number of seaside resorts as well as the pretty harbour of Cockwood. Inland two principal river valleys are followed, the Kenn and Dawlish Water. This is an area in which the wealth of past eras has been lavished on fine country estates, their houses, and gatehouses and it is easy to see why it was so popular amongst the privileged classes.

Map: OS Landranger 192 Exeter & Sidmouth (GR 958833).

Starting point: The car park in the centre of Kenton, which is located on the A379, five miles south of Exeter. Turn in towards the church and turn left into the car park by the war memorial.

Refreshments: Adjacent to the car park in Kenton are two village pubs. In addition, pubs can be found in Kenn, Dawlish, and Cockwood. There is a large selection of cafés in Dawlish and one at Powderham Castle.

The route: The outward section of the ride to Haydon and the return ride from Dawlish Water are mostly flat; the middle section has a number of relatively small hills of a reasonable gradient. As a very short and easy option, it is possible to return from point 3. This section of the ride neither uses nor crosses any main roads; however, the country lanes are of variable width and surface quality. The full distance passes through the bustling seaside town of Dawlish and includes some short sections of the busy coastal A-road.

Public Transport: There is a choice of locations at which to join the route, with railway stations at Dawlish, Dawlish Warren, and Starcross; all are on the Exeter to Plymouth main line.

---

1. **Turn L** out of the car park and follow the lane past the church, keeping straight on at the strange junction at the church gate. Shortly after passing the church, **turn R** into Chiverstone Road, the last of the three roads to the right on the left-hand bend. The lane climbs gently into rural countryside and on to an unmarked T-junction; here **turn L**. Across to your right on the wooded ridge is the

Dawlish where the stream runs out under the railway line to the sea

belvedere on the Powderham estate. The lane borders the Kenn valley to a large grass triangle, where you **turn R** and descend, crossing the River Kenn. At Wilsworthy Cross, **turn L** onto the valley road.

2. Shortly the road brings you into the charming village of Kenn. Just before the church, **turn L** (Ley Arms Cross, named after the pub on the junction). Cross the Kenn river, and **turn L** at the large grass triangle into a lane that follows the other side of the valley downstream. This section of the stream is festooned with weeping willow trees.

Eventually the road turns away from the river into a tributary valley, under the shadow of Great Haldon. **Swing L** at the dead-end sign for Haydon, effectively turning off what is the major road. Cross the small stream and follow it up the valley. At the grass triangle **keep R** towards and past the thatched cottage.

(For an easier, but less interesting route **turn L** here.)

Immediately after passing the cottage, the road swings to the left for a steady climb through Haydon Wood to Haydon Common. After the sharp left-hand bend at the

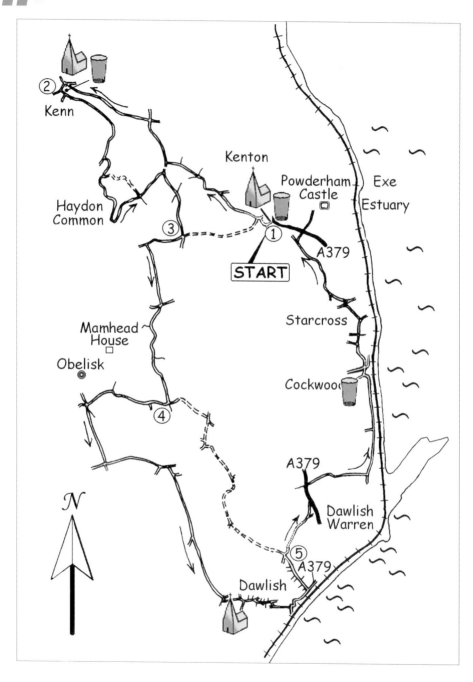

summit, enjoy the descent to the T-junction, where the short cut joins from the left. **Turn R** and descend to the next T-junction, **turn R** again and immediately climb the small hill; the views soon open out across Kenton parish.

3. At the first crossroads, located on the top of a small rise, **turn R** for Oxton and enter the rolling foothills of Mamhead parish.

(For the short and easy option, **turn L** here and follow the lane into Kenton.)

Descend into the valley and **turn L** for Mamhead at the dead-end sign, to climb to the B3381 (Ivy Cottage Cross). Cross **straight over** for Mamhead and climb up through a cutting; note the graffiti carved into the rock face. The route now bounds the old Mamhead Estate and passes many fine properties.

4. The road ends at a crossroads (Shirwells Cross).

(For a shorter return route, **turn L** for Dawlish. At the T-junction (Newhouse Cross) **turn R** for Dawlish, almost immediately **turn R** on a left-hand bend (Basket Lodge) for Haldon and Ashcombe and before the road climbs **turn L** on a right-hand bend and follow the road all the way to point 5 below.)

To follow the main route **turn R** for half a mile of gentle climbing.

Continue to the crossroads and **turn L** for a sweeping descent into the valley of Dawlish Water.

Turn L at the T-junction and follow the valley to Dawlish. Just as the road enters the town and widens on the steep descent, **turn L** for the town centre. **Turn L** at the next T-Junction into Old Town Street and follow the road past the shops to the next T-Junction. **Turn L** again into a one-way street alongside the town green.

Keep in the left-hand lane to **turn L** onto the A379 for Exeter. This can be a busy road but there are pavements on this ¼ mile section. Shortly after the zebra crossing **turn L** into Elm Road.

5. After passing Gatehouse Primary School, ignore the no through road sign, as Secmaton Lane is now a cycle path. The bollards that mark each end of the path may prove difficult for the largest of trailers. From the end of the cycle path, follow the lane to the A379 and **turn L**. After ¼ mile, take the first **R turn**, into Shutterton Lane, which is opposite the entrance to Langdon Hospital. The lane meets the coast at Dawlish Warren, opposite the Dawlish Sands campsite; **turn L** here. (Or, to visit the beach, the nature reserve, and the resort **turn R**.)

Once past the holiday parks the road runs alongside the Plymouth to Paddington rail line which divides the road from the Exe estuary. Take care, as this road can be busy at times.

The road enters Cockwood on a sharp bend, and there, in an instant, laid out before you is the charming harbour, bounded by the main rail line. Note how boats have to enter the harbour through the bridges under the railway. Ride around the harbour **turn R** onto the main road and immediately **turn L** into New Road. Cycle round the golf pitch and putt area, continuing to the **L turn** into Brickyard Lane, located opposite Starcross Primary School.

Take the second **turning L** into Witcombe Lane, which is located shortly after a sharp right-hand bend and just before a 30 mph speed restriction sign. After the second rise the road enters the 30 mph zone for Kenton.

(To visit Powderham take the first **turn R** and descend to and across the A379. Follow the drive for the castle or bear right for the café and shop. To return to the car park from the Castle **turn R** on to the A379 and descend into the village **turning L** in the bottom of the dip just after the pub.)

Alternatively follow the lane into Kenton, keeping right to the car park.

DAWLISH

The symbol for the town of Dawlish is a black swan, and if you take time to walk beside the burbling stream you are quite likely to see this bird, together with ducks and other wildfowl. The town itself is named after the river and now the banks of the river are landscaped and known as `the lawn'. The authors Jane Austen and Charles Dickens were both fond of Dawlish, indeed it was the birthplace of Dickens' hero Nicholas Nickleby.

KENTON

Standing in the pleasant village of Kenton, it is hard to believe that in the year of 1856 half the buildings were destroyed by a fire which swept through the cob and thatch structures. Having survived the fire, the fine red sandstone church, which dates from 1360, still commands the centre of the village. The church is well worth a visit, first savouring the fine entrance.

POWDERHAM

On the edge of the village of Kenton is the Powderham estate. At its entrance is a café and shop. The castle was built for Sir Philip Courtenay in the early 15th century. Over the first three centuries of its existence, the setting of the castle was rather different, with the Kenn and Exe rivers extending towards the south and east walls respectively. The Kenn receded, and an embankment was built on the Exe estuary; now the railway line mostly obscures the view of the estuary. The level grounds are home to deer. The castle has remained in the ownership of the Courtenays, who since 1553 have been Earls of Devon. It is open to the public but has quite limited hours.

9
North-east Dartmoor

17 miles

Cycling around the north-eastern fringe of Dartmoor is a delight, with its array of country lanes, bubbling streams, and villages of robust granite-walled and thatched cottages. This corner of the national park is also very high, making for rewarding panoramic views over Dartmoor and out across the lowlands. Along the route are gardens to be explored, an ancient burial chamber, and a castle; and there are plenty of opportunities to walk on the open moor or to paddle in a moorland stream. Don't forget, too, to look out for Dartmoor ponies on the moorland section of the ride.

Map: OS Landranger 191 Okehampton & North Dartmoor (GR 685925).

Starting point: On the old A30, to the western end of Whiddon Down, is a long lay-by on the west-bound side, opposite the Dartmoor View campsite. If this lay-by is full, then continue; there are a number of other, large lay-bys further on. The old A30 runs west from the roundabout on the main A30 at Whiddon Down, which is between Exeter and Okehampton.

Refreshments: Near the start is the Post Inn and the A30 services, with café, garage, and shop. Pubs are also available in Wonson, South Zeal, and South Tawton. There is a shop in Throwleigh.

The route: The route is all on minor roads, except for half a mile at the start on a rural A-road and the final section, which uses the old A30, now declassified to a minor road but remaining wide. The minor roads are typical of Devon, with varying widths and surface quality. There are a few long hills on the route, although the steeper hills in the area have been avoided.

Public Transport: A seasonal train service operates to Okehampton from Exeter. The station is approximately four miles along the old A30 from South Zeal.

---

1. **Turn R** from the lay-by to head towards Whiddon Down and almost immediately take the **first R turn** by an old garage that is now the Moorlands Farm Shop. At the T-junction, **turn R** on to the A382 and enter the Dartmoor National Park. After a third of a mile **turn L** on a right-hand bend (Toll House Cross). Fine views along the eastern edge of the national park open out on this road. Take the **first R** turn for Spinsters' Rock (Spinsters' Rock Cross).

The road rises steadily, and the splendour of Cosdon Hill soon appears in front as the brow of the hill is reached. Cosdon Hill, one of the more prominent hills when viewed from the north or east, marks the north-eastern corner of Dartmoor. The route passes right under the shadow of this hill when approaching South Zeal. Below to the left is the upper Teign valley opening out towards Chagford.

As the road starts descending, look out for the kissing gate to the left, which is on the chicane in the road. It is here that access is gained to Spinsters' Rock. After viewing the rock, proceed down the beech-lined road to the delightful little thatched cottage with its six arched windows.

Cycling near Spinsters' Rock

Cross the small stream to the A382 (Sandygate Cross), and go **straight over** the staggered junction for Gidleigh, taking care, as this is quite a blind junction. Climb another small rise and enjoy even better views that can be glimpsed through field gateways.

Take the first **turning R**, for Gidleigh, which is at Monks Withecombe Gallery; the gallery is in the courtyard on the right. Cross **straight over** the next crossroads for Gidleigh and rise to the mast on the hill. Ignore the left turn to Gidleigh keeping straight on for Wonson. The road rises onward towards the high hills of Dartmoor, but then dips down to a little

stream. At the bottom of the hill, **fork L** on the right-hand bend for Chapple before crossing the stream.

2. Turn L upon reaching the T-junction (Chapple Cross) for Gidleigh. Halfway up the hill to the moor is an ideal place to take a break; **turn left** into Gidleigh to view the ruined castle and the church. The castle is in a private garden, but can be viewed through the old arched gateway. The road into this hamlet is level.

Turn R at the grass triangle for Moortown. Ignore the right turn to Wonson at Moortown Cross, but follow the lane instead across the cattle grid, and finally you will have reached the open moor.

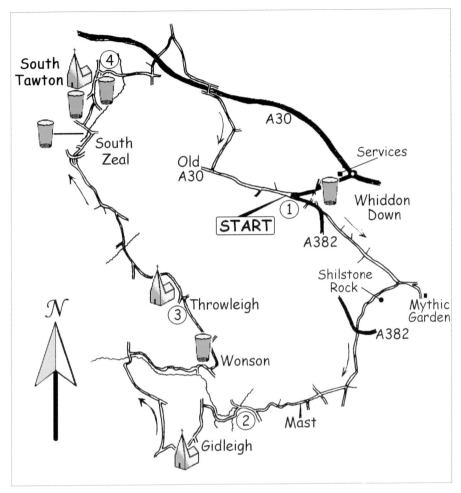

Immediately before the road rises sharply, **turn R** (Ash Green) into the side road for Ash and Wonson. This is now a lovely run down by the stream, with plenty of opportunities to cool those hot feet in the clear Dartmoor Water or to picnic under the canopy of the trees. There is also a large open area of grass where children can play. Cross the cattle grid into narrow stone-walled lanes and pass through the tiny hamlet of Ash. Go down to the T-junction and **turn L** for Wonson and Throwleigh. At the triangle just before the phonebox, **turn L** for Wonson, passing the Northmore Arms. This lane leads to the charming little Dartmoor village of Throwleigh.

3. Turn L for South Zeal at the T-junction marked by a stone cross and follow the road round to the right in front of the church into a dip and up a stiff climb to return across a cattle grid to the open moor. A short distance before the T-junction with the old A30, **turn L** to pass under the old A-road and into South Zeal. At the minor T-junction in the village **turn R** and drop to the T-junction at the bottom of the village. **Turn L** to climb the main street as far as St Mary's church; **turn R** here to pass the village school, noting the wonderful clock tower. **Turn L** at the T-junction (School Lane Cross) for South Tawton, climbing gently to the next T-junction; here **turn R** for South Tawton.

4. Ignore the first two turns to the right in South Tawton but **turn R** opposite the gable end of the church into a minor road and then **turn L** at the T-junction to leave the village and cross the stream.

The road rises now to Whiddon Down. Take the first **L turn** (Oxenham Manor Cross) for Spreyton (note the old stone cross on the opposite gatepost). Cross the A30 and enjoy the views once more. **Turn R** at the T-junction; then, where the road widens on the brow of the hill, **turn R** across the A30 and then **turn L** at the T-junction on the opposite side. Drop into the dip across the head of the river valley for the final climb of the ride. **Turn L** at the T-junction (Livaton Cross) for Whiddon Down.

● ●

SOUTH TAWTON

In the centre of the village of South Tawton stands a circular wall upon which an oak tree rises. It is said that the previous tree, an elm, had stood there since 1688, but it was replaced in 1984, having died of Dutch elm disease. The walls were originally built during the reign of Queen Elizabeth I and were rebuilt to commemorate the coronation of Queen Elizabeth II. In the church are memorials to the Oxenham family. Local legend tells of a horned white bird that appeared to 14 different dying members of this family betwen 1618 and 1892. It is said that if the bird was to look at the ailing person then the bird would take the disease away, but if the bird should look away then death would follow.

SPINSTERS' ROCK

Spinsters' Rock is a dolmen, a Neolithic burial chamber, erected around 3500-2500 BC. It is thought to have contained many burials and would have originally been covered by a long earth mound. The capstone is approximately 6 ft above ground and is nearly 15 ft long, weighing an estimated 16 tons. It is also recorded that the dolmen was encircled by stones, though there are no traces of them now. Tradition has it that the stones were originally erected by three spinsters one morning before breakfast, these ladies not being unmarried, but spinners of yarn. Public access is allowed to Spinsters' Rock despite its setting in a field which is generally occupied by horses.

10
The Otter valley
15 or 19 miles

The Otter valley has been a favourite amongst cyclists for years, with its quiet byways passing through many picturesque villages and past numerous fine houses and farms. Set between the hills of West Hill and Woodbury Common to the west and East Hill and coastal cliffs to the east, the river Otter, once a navigable river, runs down in its wide flood plain from Ottery St Mary. The towns and villages on its banks have a rich history. Sir Walter Raleigh's birthplace is adjacent to the route, as is Bicton Gardens and Agricultural College. Take your time on this ride to appreciate why these roads have proved so popular.

Map: OS Landranger 192 Exeter & Sidmouth (GR 073820).

Starting point: Lime Kiln pay-and-display car park by the mouth of the river Otter in Budleigh Salterton. Follow the B3178 to the seaward end of the town and find the car park adjacent to the beach.

Refreshments: There are plenty of pubs, cafés and ice cream outlets in Budleigh Salterton. En-route you will pass pubs in East Budleigh, Newton Poppleford, Tipton St John, and Otterton. The pub in Otterton also serves as the post office and general store, with ice creams available to eat in the beer garden. There is a café in the grounds of Bicton Gardens.

The route: Using mostly minor roads, some of which are very narrow, the route is generally rolling in nature. There are no steep hills; indeed I rode the route with my 7 and 3 year-old children on the tandem. Towards the end of the ride, the route incorporates a closed road; the surface is not perfect, as there is no through traffic to disperse the soil that washes onto it from the fields, and there is also one very narrow section. At mid-distance there is the opportunity to shorten the ride just a little, while detours on the way out will give you the opportunity to see Bicton Gardens and the birthplace of Sir Walter Raleigh.

Public Transport: The nearest railway station is at Exmouth. There is a signed cycle route on an old railway line from Exmouth to Budleigh Salterton. Where the track joins the B3178 turn left, the first left turn is the lane to East Budleigh on the route.

1. Opposite the entrance to the car park is Salting Hill, which is to be climbed to reach the town centre, the top is marked by a cross from which there is a great view. **Turn L** at the T-junction here to descend to the beach and the town centre.

(Alternatively walk along the seawall which runs between the car park and the beach and listen for the sound of the sea on both sides of you; the echo is caused by the sandstone cliffs above. Toilets can be found along here. Go through a gap in the railing to rejoin the road.)

Ride into and through the quaint town centre. At the end of the shopping street **turn R** at the traffic lights for Newton Poppleford. Cycle past a pleasant open park to your left and **fork L** into Moor Lane to stay alongside the park. The road bears round to the right, past St Peters C of E School, where the road changes to Barn Lane. At the next right hand bend **turn L**, to stay in Barn Lane, and ride out of the village.

At the T-junction **turn R** onto the B3178 and up an open climb; at the apex **turn L** into an unsigned minor road which continues to climb a little further. The good news is that the worst hill of the day is now behind you. Where the view opens out, the obelisk that stands before you is a folly in the grounds of Bicton House; the large building to its left is the house itself. The village in the foreground is East Budleigh, which can be found at the bottom of the next descent. At the T-junction under the shade of the horse chestnut trees **turn L** into Middle Street. After the village school, the road becomes High Street.

After crossing the stream, the next lane to the left is Hayes Lane, which leads to the birthplace of Sir Walter Raleigh. The farmhouse can be found a mile up this lane.

Continue through the village, past the church and climb out into a wide valley. The road soon descends to the gates to Bicton Arena; unfortunately there is no access here to Bicton House.

East Budleigh

50

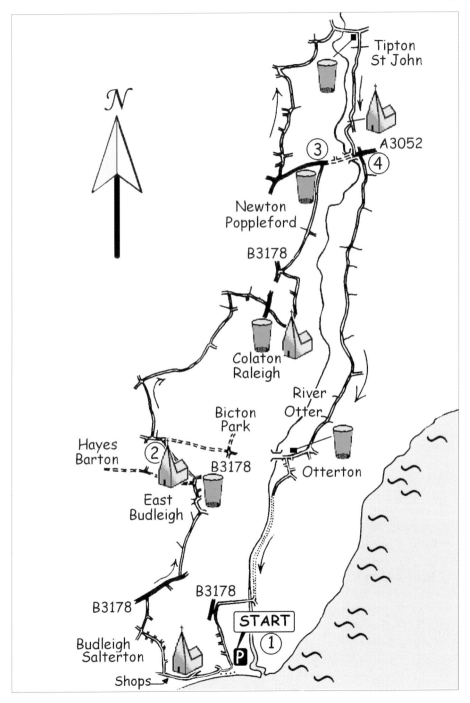

(To visit these Botanical Gardens **turn R** back on yourself immediately before the Bicton Arena gates (Sandy Cross) and over the hill past the obelisk to the Brick Cross roads and **turn L** onto the B3178, Bicton Gardens is on the left after ⅓ mile. After your visit retrace to the Bicton Arena gates.)

2. Immediately after the gates **turn R** for another gentle, but steady rise. From the top you can see Woodbury Common, on the skyline ahead. **Turn R** at the crossroads (Stowford Cross). For much of this road there is a wall on the right, which is the boundary wall of the Bicton estate. After the wall has been left behind the road swings to the right; **fork L** here, and after a gentle descent keep straight on to the T-junction opposite Pophams Farm. **Turn R** in to Colaton Raleigh, and **turn R** again at the T-junction with the B3178, taking care, as this is a blind junction. Almost immediately take the first **L turn**, into Church Road; on the junction is a memorial stone to Queen Victoria.

Descend into the old village. Look out for the no through road sign located just before the village hall and **turn L** here into Shepherds Lane. The road promptly climbs a little but the reward is the first views through the hedgerow of the Otter river valley. This very narrow lane ends at a T-junction near the B-road; **turn R**, away from the B-road to Dotton. Eventually this

road runs into Newton Poppleford and drops down to the A3052.

(To reduce the length of the ride, **turn R** and descend to cross the river Otter, and then take the first road on the right to follow the river valley for Otterton (point 4 below).)

3. **Turn L** and ride through the village. Just before the mini roundabout, **turn R** for Venn Ottery. Unfortunately there is a steep section extending for about 30 yards on this road, but thereafter it is downhill all the way. After swinging round to the right through Venn Ottery, the road goes on to Tipton St John. At the T-junction by the church **turn R** and cross the river Otter. Shortly after passing the pub, **turn R** into Hayne Lane in the direction of Newton Poppleford. Take the **right fork** along this delightful lane to stay close to the river.

4. At the T-junction with the A3052, **turn L** and then immediately **turn R** to continue to follow the river valley for Otterton. Extreme caution is required on this staggered crossroads. After a number of farms, a long and gradual climb away from the valley floor arrives at a T-junction. **Turn R** here and enjoy freewheeling into the picturesque village of Otterton. Shortly after the pub and post office, **turn L** opposite the village green to start climbing Maunders Hill. At the last of the houses on

Cycling along the lanes in the Otter Valley

the right **turn R**, just before the de-restricted sign, into a road that is signed 'road closed'.

This road was closed because of subsidence and at its narrowest point is no more than about a yard in width. Since it is rarely used by motorists, it is a beautiful lane to cycle along, with the lower Otter valley viewed though the mature wooded bank that marks the boundary of the flood plain. After the road descends out of the trees, **turn R** at the T-junction to cross the flood plain. The end of this flat crossing is marked by a sharp left-hand bend and a short ramp up. At the T-junction at the top of the rise **turn L** into Granary Lane on the outskirts of Budleigh Salterton, away from the B-road. The route is now predominantly downhill all the way back to the car park, which can be found on

the left just before reaching the sea.

● ●

BICTON
Between 1818 and 1836, a gardener by the name of John Claudius Loudon engineered a solution for a greenhouse which he constructed at the gardens where he was the head gardener. Twenty years later his ideas for the Bicton Palmhouse were expanded by William Paxton at Kew Gardens. The original palmhouse of Loudon's can still be admired at Bicton Botanical Gardens.

EAST BUDLEIGH
A mile along Hayes Lane in the charming village of East Budleigh is the Tudor farmhouse of Hayes Barton, in which Sir Walter Raleigh was born in 1552, and in All Saints' church the first pew on the north side of the nave bears the Raleigh family coat of arms. Although it is hard to believe now, at the time Raleigh grew up in East Budleigh it was an old and decaying riverside port.

East Devon excursion

7 or 26 miles

Between the ridges stretching from the Blackdown Hills to the north and the sea to the south are a number of tributary rivers feeding the river Axe, which in their passing have cut deep valleys into these hills. There is a grand scale to the landscape here, added to which the wealth of past generations has left a legacy of fine buildings. The ridge top roads offer ideal routes for cycling, as they are relatively level and offer some great views. Best of all, however, is the descent, which barring a couple of minor interruptions, continues from the midway point of the route to the finish.

Map: OS Landranger 193 Taunton & Lyme Regis (GR 247939); most of the route is also on sheet 192 Exeter & Sidmouth.

Starting point: The car park in the centre of the village of Colyton, which is located one mile up the B3161 from Colyford, between Sidmouth and Lyme Regis on the A3052. Parking charges apply seven days a week. Toilets are available at the car park.

Refreshments: The only pubs on the route are in Colyton. There are however cafés at Colyton, on the way to the tramway and at the tramway, and on the climb to Stockland Hill at Burrow Farm, a short drop from the road.

The route: There are two distinct sections of this route: the low lying roads on the edge of the flood plains, and the ridge roads. The climb between the two is quite long, but fortunately it is broken into stages and there are no steep gradients. There are a few main roads to be crossed, plus two short sections of main road to be ridden, the busier being about 300 yards of the A30. A very short and fairly easy option is available by returning from point 2.

Public Transport: The nearest railway station is in Honiton. From the station proceed straight up the long and steep hill; the road that enters from the left at the top of the hill is at point 4 on the route.

---

1. Turn R out of the car park into Dolphin Street to descend out of the village. Immediately after crossing the river Coly, **fork R** for the Seaton tramway.

(To visit the Seaton Tramway, **take first left fork** into Kinsgdon.)

Otherwise continue along the lane, passing the 'liable to flooding sign'.

A tram departing from Colyton station

This lane follows the tramway line and even passes under it – so look out for sightings of the tram as you travel along. The lane emerges by the level crossing at Colyford; here **turn L** onto the A3052 and pass through the boundary gateposts for Colyford. Cross the river Axe and continue past Boshill Cross, then almost immediately **turn L** for Lower Bruckland; this is just before the main road really starts to climb.

Just after the fishery, **turn L** at the grass triangle for Musberry. **Turn L** at the T-junction for The Street. Cross **straight over** the A358 in the direction of Whitford. Follow the road through the village of Whitford, passing under the main Exeter to Waterloo railway line and climb to a T-junction.

(For the seven mile ride **turn L** here for Colyton and follow the road over some small hillocks to a T-junction; **turn R** to descend sharply into Colyton.)

2. **Turn R** for Shute. This was previously a B-road and is therefore well known to locals and carries more traffic than the lanes used up until now. Descend to the now defunct railway station and hotel that was Seaton Junction and then **fork L** into a narrow minor road; **bear R** by the railway bridge. **Keep R** at the next T-junction and climb to the T-junction with the downgraded B-road (Boarscroft Cross) **turn L** for Shute.

Climb up past the imposing gatehouse to the Shute estate. The

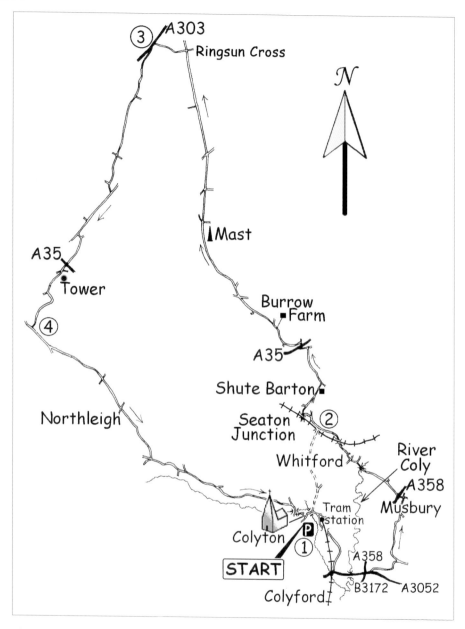

climb thereafter eases as the road ascends to the A35. This is a busy tourist route; so take care in crossing. **Turn R** onto the main road and then immediately **turn L** for Dalwood and Stockland. This is the second stage of the climb and passes Burrow Farm

Gardens on the right. The final section to the summit is the longest haul. The crest is marked by the great mast on Stockland Hill. Follow this road to the fourth crossroads (Ringsun Cross), at Colystock Kitchens, reached after a long shallow incline. **Turn L.**

3. At the A30, **turn L** for about 300 yards of shallow descent, but take care as this is a very busy trunk road. Take the first **fork L** for Cotleigh and climb a small rise; this is the ridge to the east of the Sid valley. From here the ride to Colyton is downhill almost all of the way. At the T-junction, **turn R** for Honiton and proceed through the trees. In the next wooded area, **turn L** for Axminster; the turning (take care not to miss it) is just before the lane starts to descend from the ridge to Honiton. Where the road rises slightly to the A35 at Tower Cross (named after nearby Bishops Tower), cross straight over, with caution as this is a very busy road.

4. The gentle rise continues to a T-junction; here **turn L** for Northleigh. The descent continues steeply to a crossroads (Farwood Cross), which is located just before a right-hand bend; **turn L** here for Colyton. The road finally reaches the valley floor, crossing a small stream, and then promptly climbs again.

Cross the Coly river and then **fork L** into Vicarage Street. Shortly **turn**

L, opposite the monumental gates of Colyton House, into Rosemary Lane. Take the **R fork** just after the Gerrard Arms into Lower Church Street and admire the fine church tower. At the T-junction opposite the Kingfisher freehouse **turn R** to go back to the car park.

• •

COLYTON

The octagonal lantern on the church tower at Colyton cannot fail to get your attention. Built in the 15th century on top of the Norman tower, it was intended as a navigational light to aid boats approaching from the Axe estuary. There are few other examples of such lanterns, Boston Stump in Lincolnshire and Ely cathedral perhaps being the best known. In the early 16th century this was the fourth wealthiest town in Devon. The town once had a number of tanneries, which supplied leather to locally stationed armies. The last remaining oak bark tannery in the country can now be found at the bottom of King Street.

SEATON TRAMWAY

In 1966, following Dr Beeching's report, the branch line to Seaton, Colyford, and Colyton to Seaton Junction was closed. On the bed of that railway now runs the tramway linking Colyton to the seaside at Seaton. The tramway was opened in 1970 and operates many purpose-built trams which replicate the models that were a common site in towns and cities around the country. The journey lasts 30 minutes, and there is a choice of open-top cars, from which fine views of the Axe valley can be enjoyed to the full, or single-deck saloons, that offer shelter from the elements.

12

Culm Valley and Blackdown Hills

11 or 21 miles

The Culm river valley carves deep into the Blackdown Hills. The waters have turned many ancient wheels to generate power for various industries over the years. There are a few remaining signs of this past industry to be seen along the way, but principally the valley is a rural delight, with fertile farmland rising up steeply to the ridges that bound the valley. From the summit of the ridge included in this route are views stretching across west Somerset. There is a chance to visit the landmark obelisk of the Wellington Monument, as well as Coldharbour Mill and Hemyock Castle – just two of the attractions of the towns of Uffculme, Culmstock, and Hemyock, that grew up on the edges of the Culm flood plain.

Map: OS Landranger 181 Minehead & Brendon Hills (GR 066067).

Starting point: The square in Uffculme, which has limited car parking. The village is to the east of the M5. Leave at junction 27 and follow the A38 to Waterloo Cross; here turn right onto the B3181, following the signs to the left to Uffculme.

Refreshments: In addition to the facilities at the start there are a number of pubs at regular intervals on the route, in Culmstock, Hemyock, and on the monument ridge. There are no cafés on the route; however, there are shops and a fish and chip shop in Hemyock.

The route: The route climbs its way along the Culm river valley until it ascends alongside a tributary valley onto the monument ridge of the Blackdown Hills. The B-roads carry local traffic, after which the country lanes onto the ridge are quiet, and thankfully longer than they are steep. The ridge road is wide and straight and carries local traffic. The return route follows a quiet steep narrow lane and then follows the Culm on the other bank in quiet narrow twisting lanes. The ride can be shortened by turning at Hemyock, thus avoiding the climb to the ridge.

Public Transport: The nearest railway station is Tiverton Parkway. Sustrans route 3 can be followed from the station to the roundabout to the north of Willand and from here there is a level B-road to Uffculme.

1. Drop out of the lower side of the square, towards and past the spired church, descending further to cross the river. Follow the road as it twists its way through the fertile lowlands of the Culm and its feeder streams. On approaching Culmstock, the Blackdown Hills can be seen rising before you.

Hemyock's cast-iron street light

As the road arrives in Culmstock it swings sharply down to the left; look out for the first crossroads on this descent and **turn R** into Fore Street and the B3391 for Hemyock. Ride past the Ilminster Stage Inn on the right and the church, which has a yew tree on top of the tower, to your left. Follow the road to Hemyock and look out for the castle on your right as you drop into the village. This medieval stronghold is open to the public by prior appointment, telephone 01823 680745. Continue with the church, the Catherine Wheel pub, and the village pump on your right.

2. Eventually descend to the river crossing, (Note the raised plank walkway for use in times of flooding; it looks as though it would be quite tricky with a bike,

however.) **Turn R** at the site of the former milk factory, now a new housing development, into Lower Millhayes for Clayhidon and Lowerstanton.

(For the shortcut continue to the first turning to the **left** (Withy Lane Cross) for Culm Pine and Whitehall and follow the route to Whitehall (point 4 below).)

Follow the lane out of the town and eventually cross the river to the T-junction (Byes Cross). **Turn L** for Clayhidon and Churchstanton. Now you can really enjoy lush green Culm Valley as you while your way along the peaceful twisting country lanes. Shortly after the crossroads, **turn L** into the first side road for Clayhidon and cross the river Culm again, rising past the delightful, thatched Hidon Mill and up to Clayhidon parish hall. **Turn R** here into the side road.

At the T-junction opposite Hidewood Farm, **turn L** and start up the long climb; it is a mostly twisting narrow road at a reasonable gradient and is best tackled at a gentle pace. At the T-junction, which marks the top, **turn R** for Taunton and Pidminster.

3. Descend along the ridge edge to the crossroads at the Merry Harriers pub and **turn L**.

The road climbs gently. Where it descends, it passes Quarts Moor,

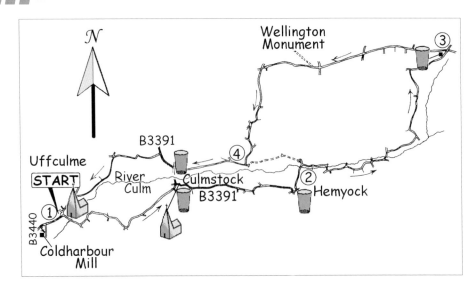

which is owned by the National Trust and from which there is an excellent view across Wellington in Somerset and on to the Quantock Hills. Soon after views of the obelisk can be snatched across the field to the right. Look out for the Wellington Monument car park on the right just after the crossroads for Wellington. From the car park there is a ½ mile rough track leading to the monument.

To continue on the ride, proceed straight past the car park and into the dip to a wide junction on a sharp right-hand bend. **Turn L** into the wide junction and immediately **turn L again** into a minor road for Culmstock.

4. At the bottom of the long descent is a T-junction opposite a thatched cottage. **Turn R** here for Culmstock and Tiverton. Follow the river valley road down to

Culmstock, arriving opposite the school. Join the B3391 towards Wellington and Tiverton, which is effectively **straight on**. The Culm Valley Inn is by the river crossing to the left. Halfway up the hill, **turn L** into a minor road for Prescott and proceed through this farming hamlet to the T-junction. **Turn L** here for Uffculme. **Turn L** at the next T-junction and follow the road into Uffculme arriving in the village square.

• •

HEMYOCK

It was in the small rural centre of Hemyock that a collection of farming teenagers joined a club called the Calf Club. In 1920 the dairy purchased a heifer calf for each teenager. The animals had above average milk yield and their introduction to the local herds improved the standard of the local dairy stock. The need for such an organisation in rural areas was acknowledged, and similar groups sprang up in Hampshire and

Leicestershire, the Daily Mail then sponsored the club and from it grew the Young Farmers, as it is known today. Meanwhile the dairy, which was established after the First World War, was acquired by St Ivel and produced the 'Gold' brand of butter.

The curiosity of the village, to be found on a junction opposite the church, is the cast-iron street lamp incorporating the village pump. Behind the church is the castle, a fortified house dating back to the 14th century. It has very limited opening hours but can be viewed by prior appointment (see point 1).

UFFCULME

The market town of Uffculme is to be found on the western bank of the Culm river. The centre of the village square is marked by the shambles, which dates from the 17th century. This is a timber structure that now contains seats and it was here that the village butcher would once have slaughtered and prepared his stock; that is, until 1914, when the market closed. The main source of employment in the village was its woollen mill, Coldharbour Mill. It was first a paper mill in 1700; then it was converted to grind corn in 1753, and finally it operated as a woollen mill from 1797 until 1981, when it became a working wool museum, in which you can view waterwheels, steam engines, and textile machinery in action, etc.

WELLINGTON MONUMENT

The 175 ft high Wellington Monument stands on the north-western edge of the Blackdown Hills, just inside Somerset. It

The Wellington Monument

appears as a great boundary post to travellers way down below in their high speed metal boxes on the M5 and A38. Plans to build the obelisk were made in response to the Duke of Wellington's victory at Waterloo. The foundation stone was laid in 1817, but the plans proved too elaborate for the money available. It was after the death of the Iron Duke in 1852 that the work recommenced, but took a further 40 years to complete. It has been in the ownership of the National Trust since 1933.

Villages and hamlets of the Clyst valley

16 or 23 miles

To the east of the river Clyst is a fertile low-lying area in which there is a web of streams and brooks that all find their way to the Clyst. Defining the eastern limit of this area, the land rises to a relatively low ridge that runs from north to south. Land use here is predominantly agricultural, with many farms, stables, and orchards. In addition to the charming villages and substantial farmsteads, there are numerous thatched cottages that typify the usual concept of picturesque Devon scenery. Unless journeying to one of the villages or hamlets, there is little reason to pass through these twisting roads, making this a fine area for cycling.

Map: OS Landranger 192 Exeter & Sidmouth (GR 983972).

Starting point: The Green, a free public car park located behind Broadclyst village green. Turn off the B3181 Exeter to Cullompton road opposite the Red Lion Inn and adjacent to the thatched bus shelter; then turn right into a dead end and keep right around the green.

Refreshments: There are no cafés on the route, but pubs can be found in Broadclyst, Plymtree, Talaton, and Whimple, and there are shops in Broadclyst, Talaton and Whimple.

The route: The route is entirely on minor roads, with a section of downgraded B-road between Aunk and Langford Green and also a short section at Talaton. Some of the lanes are very narrow. The route is as close to level as you will find in Devon, with no large hills. There is the opportunity to take a shortcut at Aunk, which makes for an even flatter route.

Public Transport: There is a railway station at Whimple, which is on the Exeter Central–London Waterloo line.

---

1. Follow the road round to the left out of the car park and past the village green; then **turn R** at the T-junction opposite the bold pink thatched cottages. Follow the lane out of the village, passing Marker's Cottage, a medieval cob house, now owned by the National Trust.

Avoid forking left on the sharp right-hand bend, but proceed instead to the crossroads and **turn L**. Following a short climb **turn L** for Westwood and Clyst St Lawrence at the grass triangle.

Cycling past a cider orchard on the outskirts of Whimple

The wooded hill rising away to your left is Ashclyst Forest, which is maintained by the National Trust and has a network of pleasant walks.

Drop into the dip and cross the bridge, shortly after which **turn R** for Ashclyst opposite more brightly coloured cottages. The lane soon crosses back over the stream and then twists and turns as it makes its way past a number of wayside farms and cottages. At the T-junction **turn R**; climb gently to the next T-junction and **turn L** for Clyst St Lawrence. The lane rises, then falls; after it levels out take the first **turning L**, shortly after passing Hitts Barton Equestrian Centre. At the T-junction under the humming pylons **turn R** for

Talaton. The road passes through the wonderfully named Aunk and joins the old B-road at a T-junction (Aunk Cross).

(For the shortcut to Talaton, **turn R** and follow the old B-road to point 4 below.)

2. To proceed on the route **turn L** for Clyst Hydon. Continue through the village and up a small climb the other side. Take the first **turning R** (Langford Green Cross) into a minor road at a large, overgrown green triangle. On arrival opposite the church at Plymtree, **turn L** at the T-junction and go through Norman's Green. (There are no signs to tell you where you are, just a chapel on the crossroads.) Continue across a shallow river valley to a T-junction.

3. **Turn R** onto the ridge road. This does not feel particularly like a ridge; it is, however, as high as it gets between the river Tale to the left, and the feeder streams to the Clyst valley to the right. Stay on this road for approximately 3½ miles until the second crossroads (Bittery Cross). The road falls away immediately after the junction and there is a shelter and seat looking out across the Tale valley to the distant ridge of East Hill Strips. **Turn R** for Talaton and descend to the village.

4. At the T-junction opposite the timbered Talaton Inn, **turn L** for Fairmile and Ottery St Mary. Just

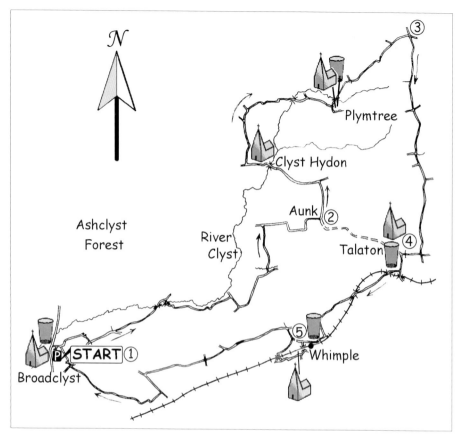

before the railway bridge **turn R** for Newtown and Whimple. As you make your way towards Whimple, crossing the railway line twice, enjoy the views across the Clyst valley towards the mid-Devon hills. At the T-junction (Perriton Cross) **turn R**, signed 'village centre'. Pass the railway station on your left, then just after the Thirsty Farmer on your right **turn L** at the roundabout signed 'village centre', passing under the railway bridge. **Turn R** immediately in front of the church; the road soon reduces to a narrow lane beside the railway.

Look out for a bridge to the right and **turn R** here to pass under the railway line and then follow the lane around to the right for Whimple again.

5. At the T-junction opposite the White House, **turn L** for Broadclyst. The village soon gives way to orchards. Continue to the first **turning L** for Rockbeare, which is by the cottage with pointed arches above its windows. Cross straight over Tubb Corner Cross, ignoring the sign to Broadclyst and **turn L** at the T-

Broadclyst church and village pub

junction. Halfway down the hill **turn R** for Elbury. The ride now finishes much as it began with a flat, narrow and twisty road. Take care to follow the highway or you may find yourself in a farmyard, as I very nearly did.

As you ride alongside the brook the bright colours of Broadclyst come into view, and so we return to the village whence we started. Just before the junction, look up to the right to see the old windmill, now defunct and unsafe. Cross **straight over** the crossroads into Green Tree Road and then **turn R** into Maple Road, where the tarmac turns to paving. At the T-junction **turn L** for the village centre. Just after School Lane on the right, **turn L** by the village green and follow the

road round to the **right** into the car park.

● ●

BROADCLYST

Broadclyst is on the Killerton estate (see route 14). It contains many fine buildings, including almshouses, cottages, the church, the school, the mill, and the pub. The village even has a stone-built thatched bus shelter, although it was only built in 1925. Behind the church, and reached through the churchyard, is Clyston Mill. This water-powered grain mill is owned by the National Trust and is open on Sunday, Monday, and Tuesday afternoons in summer.

Within the parish is a farm called Churchill, dating from before Domesday Book. This is the original home of the Churchill family, who are said to have taken their name from the farm at the time of Henry II.

65

Killerton estate, the Exe and the tributary valleys

13 or 25 miles

I f there was any doubt in my mind that this route makes its way through an active agricultural area, this was put to rest as I pedalled my way round. My son on the back of the tandem kept count and assured me that no fewer than 16 tractors passed us. The first loop goes into the Yeo river valley; this is the agricultural part, with small villages along the way. The second loop takes in the Culm river valley and the wealthier part of the Killerton estate, where the house and gardens can also be explored. The route returns via the larger villages of Bradninch and Silverton, the latter commanding views across the Exe and the Culm. The start is in the most delightful of villages, Thorverton.

Map: OS Landranger 192 Exeter & Sidmouth (GR 924022).

Starting point: The public car park to the western edge of Thorverton. The village is signed from the A396 Exeter–Tiverton road; it is to the west of the road and the car park is to the right of the right fork at the top of the main street.

Refreshments: There is a café at Killerton. Pubs can be found in Thorverton, Sweetham, Bramford Speke, Bradninch, and Silverton. Shops can be found in Bradninch and Silverton.

The route: The route is all on minor roads; with two A-road crossings. There is a mixture of very narrow and wider lanes which carry some local traffic. The route is reasonably level, though there are a few rolling hills, the hardest section being from Killerton to Silverton. There is the opportunity to split the figure of eight route into two equal parts.

Public Transport: There is a railway at Sweetham (point 2 on the route), on the Exeter to Barnstaple line.

---

1. **Turn L** out of the car park and at the T-junction which follows, immediately **turn R** for Upton Pyne. Very soon the road rises around a left-hand bend, **turn R** here for Raddon. Ride out of the village, passing the playing field and playground on your left.

Upon reaching the T-junction alongside the ancient farm of Raddon Court, **turn L** for Upton

Thorverton viewed across the stream from the green

Pyne. Soon the road rises significantly; this is the crossing from the River Exe to the River Yeo, and as you would expect extensive views soon open out. After a short descent, take the first **R turn** (Rixaford Cross), immediately before a bungalow, for Shute.

The route now follows the south facing slopes of the Yeo valley as it proceeds to a rather strange junction at which all roads are required to give way (Shute Cross); go **straight on** here for Newton St Cyres.

Descend past two left turns and then at the first crossroads (Wyke Cross), **turn L** for Newton St Cyres. Ride into Sweetham, arriving at Station Cross. The Beer Engine pub and Brewery are on the right and the railway station is down to the right.

2. Cross **straight over** here for Sweetham and Shute. At the grass triangle (Nortons Cross) **turn R** for Winscott. Then **turn L** at Winscott for Stockleigh Pomeroy and Cheriton Fitz. Take the first **turning R** for Upton Pyne. At the T-junction (Pye Corner) **turn sharp L** for Thorverton, and then **turn R** for Bramford Speke at the first crossroads, appropriately named Starved Oak, as there is a gnarled oak on the grass triangle here. After a few sharp bends take the **R turn** into an unsigned road. Beware of the unexpectedly sharp double bends and continue into the delightful village of Bramford Speke arriving at a T-junction. **Turn L** at this T-junction. There follows a

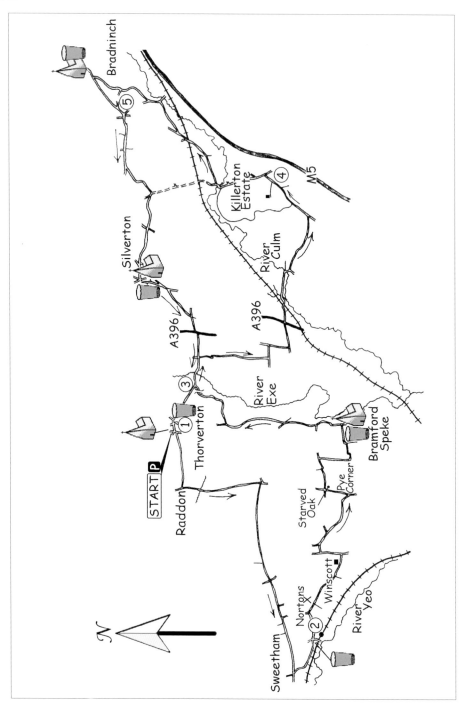

steep gravelled descent, at the bottom of which you **turn R** into an unsigned lane, identifiable by a height restriction sign.

3. Drop down to the flood plain and pass under the disused railway bridge to the T-junction (Station Cross); **turn R** for Exeter.

(This is mid-distance; to return to the start, turn left into Thorverton. Alternatively, if you are just riding the second circuit, this is where you pick up the route, having descended through the main street of Thorverton.)

Cross over the river Exe at a popular paddling spot. At the first crossroads (Batchmore Cross), **turn R** for Never Exe into a narrow road squeezed between two old houses. As you proceed, beware of the unexpectedly sharp double bend. At times when the river levels are high these roads can be subject to flooding.

At the unsigned T-junction, **turn L**, and then **turn R** for Rewe at the grass triangle on the next T-junction. Then **turn L** for Rewe at the next T-junction. Cross **straight over** the A386 at the stone cross for Columbjohn and then cross over the railway line and over two river bridges. Just before the second bridge is a pleasant grassy bank by the river, an ideal shaded spot for a paddle on a hot day. Towards the top of the climb from the river you catch the first sightings of Killerton House which, under the protection

of a wooded hill, stands in stately manner, presiding over its lands. Descend to the T-junction (Danes Cross) and **turn L** for Killerton.

4. The entrance into Killerton House is on the left, and there is a pleasant overspill car park and picnic area in the orchard to the right. Continue to the grass triangle on the T-junction and **turn L** for Silverton (although still signed as the B3185, it has been downgraded to a minor road). Climb up the small rise, and then drop to the crossing over a small stream, after which take the **R turn** for Bradninch.

(To shorten the return route to Thorverton, stay on the downgraded B-road to Silverton.)

Immediately cross a disused level crossing, followed by a bridge over a stream; then there is the steepest hill of the day. Cross the main railway line again and, shortly after the hill starts to rise, take the **R turn** (Potters Cross) for Hele, into Strathculm Road. Descend to the T-junction by the old paper factory and **turn L** for Bradninch. The road rises up into the village of Bradninch, arriving at a T-junction opposite the White Lion Inn. **Turn L** for Silverton.

5. On the edge of the village, at the apex of the small rise, **turn R** at the crossroads (Higher Hill Cross) for Silverton. This is a pleasant short winding section at a useful descending gradient; at the T-junction with the downgraded B-road **turn R** for Silverton and climb up through the shaded cutting. As the road levels, the panorama opens out across the flood plain at the confluence of the rivers Culm and Exe.

Continue to the middle of Silverton, crossing **straight over** a mini roundabout on the way. The next mini roundabout marks the centre, and there is a small green to the left. Continue **straight over** the roundabout and then almost immediately **turn L** into Exeter Road and pass the Three Tuns Inn.

Soon after leaving the village **fork R**. Descend to the T-junction (Beech Cross) and **turn R** for Thorverton. Drop down to the main A386, opposite the Ruffwell Inn. **Turn L** and then immediately **turn R** for Thorverton. Climb past the green and up the main street **turning R** at the top, the car park is then on your right.

Killerton house and drive

• •

BRADNINCH
The nearby River Culm provided the power to produce paper, and an industry soon developed that brought much wealth to this small, former wool town. The Hele mill still survives, having passed from Dewdney to Wiggins Teape and now into American ownership. Most of the farms in the parish are owned by the Duchy of Cornwall, and the town hall bears the three white ostrich feathers of the Prince of Wales, Duke of Cornwall. Alongside the feathers is the black eagle

of Richard, the second son of King John, who gave the town its charter in the 12th century.

KILLERTON
Although the Aclands made Killerton their main residence in the late 17th century, the house was completely rebuilt in the 1770s and the grounds were laid out. The Aclands owned Killerton until they handed it to the National Trust in 1944. The gardens are rather more notable than the house, with a wooded hillside, a beech grove, and Edwardian gardens.

THORVERTON
Thorverton is a delightful little village, with roadside streams said to have been introduced following an outbreak of cholera. It still has a large flour mill; it is four storeys high with five bays and is said to be the largest in Devon. The oldest part dates from 1898, and the original water turbines are still in use. There was a mill recorded here in the Domesday Book.

The Grand Western canal and the Lowman valley

19 miles

From the fertile valleys through which the Grand Western canal snakes, to the delightful Lowman river valley, there is a collection of twisting Devon lanes passing through a number of ancient villages. The return route is by way of a ridge before the descent through the estate of Knightshayes Court, now owned by the National Trust. There is plenty of scope to spot birdlife on this route so take your time and while away a day in the heart of Devon's glorious countryside.

Map: OS Landranger 181 Minehead & Brendon Hills (GR 963124).

Starting point: The pay-and-display car park for the Grand Western canal to the south of Tiverton, off the B3391; look out for the signs. This B-road is the southern ring road to the town, between the north Devon link road (A361) and the A396 Exeter road.

Refreshments: There is a café at the start of the route and there are pubs in Halberton, Sampford Peverell, and Uplowman. At Huntsham there is a post office and shop; at Knightshayes Court a National Trust café, and in Tiverton there are two cafés that you pass.

The route: Most of it is on minor roads apart from a short section of B-road on the return ride and two short sections on a downgraded B-road. There are off-road sections at the beginning of the ride (on the canal towpath) and towards the end, approaching Knightshayes, although alternative road routes have been suggested. There is also a short distance that you must walk with your bicycle in the heart of Halberton. Most of the route is fairly easy cycling; the Lowman valley is a long gentle climb. After Huntsham, however, there is the one large hill of the day.

Public Transport: The nearest railway station is Tiverton Parkway. Sustrans route 3 can be followed from the station to Sampford Courtenay, where the route can be picked up.

---

1. From the end of the car park beside the tearooms, take the ramp up to the canal. The towpath is open to cyclists, despite the contradictory signs, but pedestrians have right of way. You have to walk around the bridges and, of course, watch out for anglers and their

Horse-drawn barge on the Grand Western Canal

fishing tackle. Follow the towpath under five bridges, leaving the canal at Crown Hill Bridge and **turning R** onto the lane to cross the canal bridge. This narrow lane leads to the village of Halberton. On arriving at the T-junction opposite 'Ashleigh', **turn L**. Shortly **turn R** into Church Path.

(Alternatively, if you want to avoid the towpath, **turn L** out of the car park and follow the road to a 25% gradient sign. Part way up the climb, **turn L** into a small lane. **Swing R** at the first junction and then **turn L** at the T-junction opposite a farm building. Drop down to and ride alongside the disused railway line for a short distance to a T-junction; **turn L** and cross an old railway bridge to a 30 mph sign for Halberton. **Turn R**

into Church Path as above.) The lane soon downgrades to a footpath; so walk your bike around the church wall, passing the children's play park and turning into Pond Hill. Remount your bike to descend past the pond and up to the T-junction; **turn R**, with caution, as this is a popular road for motorists.

2. Continue to the village boundary and, just after the derestricted sign, **turn R** into a minor road, which is alongside the canal, though the canal is far higher, being on top of the bank to the left. At the T-junction (Ivy House Cross) **turn R**, away from the canal for Willand, and then take the **first L**, which is to be found under the mature oak trees. Follow the delightful twisting and

turning lane to reach Sampford Peverell, arriving with the canal laid out before you. Ignore the cycle route signs and continue on the road to a T-junction and a very sharp **L turn** to cross the canal bridge. **Turn R** immediately after the canal bridge.

Turn R shortly after the church to descend into a lane called Boobery. This narrow twisting stone-walled lane winds its way through the old village, over a small river bridge, and on through a new estate to a T-junction on the edge of the village. **Turn L** and rise gently before passing through a tunnel under the dual carriageway. Then, just as the road starts climbing, **turn L** onto a particularly narrow twisting lane, which eventually rises to the hamlet of Whitnage. **Turn L** at the T-junction into a lane leading to Uplowman.

3. **Turn R** for Huntsham at the crossroads immediately after the pub. Look out for the fine dovecote on the pub to the right. Go

73

through the village, passing the church and a few farmsteads. This is now the start of the cycling delight of the Lowman river valley. Our way is upstream and the gradient remains gentle, yet steady; so take your time and feast your senses in this wonderful valley. From the brow of the climb a substantial building, Huntsham Court, can be seen on the hillside. This neo-Gothic mansion house was built in 1870 for Charles Troyte and is now a hotel. By the Huntsham sign **turn L** into the village. Take a peek over the hedge on the right at Huntsham Court; then cross the stream and pass the charming post office, formerly the smithy. Next the big ascent of the ride commences. At the summit **bear R** and pass the rather strange radio mast, that when viewed from the distance looks like a floating bubble!

Cross **straight over** at the first crossroads, and then **turn L** at the second crossroads (Van Post Cross) for Tiverton. Follow the road across the tops of the hills, with distant views across the Exe valley to the west.

4. Soon after the road starts descending steeply, **fork R** onto a minor road which is signed as cycle route 3.

(The cycle track is a little rough for some short sections and gravelly in others. To avoid it, **continue straight on** down the hill, around

the perimeter of the estate, and on to the T-junction; **turn L** onto the route, to cross the dual carriageway or **turn R** to visit Knightshayes Court.)

Follow the very minor roadway on route 3, past the corrugated barn and then **turn L** under the trees, again signed as route 3. The road reduces to a track and generally climbs at a varying gradient to the crest of the hill. On entering the woods at Backers Down the track dips sharply away on a fine gravel-surfaced tarmac.

At the bottom of the hill the woodland route emerges into the main estate alongside Garden Cottage and the walled garden. Follow the drive around to the right and go past the house and down the drive. (If you want to visit the property, turn left past the stable block with its spire and go through the car park to find the bicycle park.)

Turn L at the bottom of the drive, following the twists and turns to cross over the dual carriageway. Descend to the outskirts of Tiverton at a T-junction and **turn R**, followed immediately by a **L turn**. Take the next **turn L** into Carew Road and follow round to the right through the housing estate. At the mini roundabout **turn L** and then immediately **turn R** into a one-way street (Chapel Street). At the T-junction at the end **turn L** and cross over the river bridge and past the clock tower to the roundabout.

(To avoid using the main road, walk over the road and up the footpath ramps to the mini roundabout. **Go straight on** up Canal Hill to the canal car park, which is on the left.)

Turn L onto the A396 and then take the first **turn R** into Old Road. Take the first **R turn** into Lodge Road and climb round the bends to the T-junction and **turn R**. Follow The Avenue to the T-junction and **turn L** into Canal Hill; the canal car park is almost immediately on the **left**.

● ● ● ● ● ● ● ● ● ● ● ● ● ● ● ● ● ● ● ●

GRAND WESTERN CANAL

Enjoy the linear country park of the Grand Western canal, that stretches from Tiverton towards Taunton. Trips, varying in length from 1 hour to 3 hours, are offered between April and October on horse-drawn barges. The canal was built in 1814, primarily for the lime kilns that can be found alongside the canal in Tiverton. Although the canal was closed for many years it survived because of the freshwater springs that naturally feed it.

The canal path is now open to cyclists. However pedestrians have the right of way and cyclists are required to walk under the narrow bridges.

HALBERTON

Halberton is separated into two parts – upper and lower – by a remarkable pond, which is served by warm water springs and is said to never freeze over. This is a tranquil area, with ducks and moorhens lazing in their naturally warmed pool. The church of St Andrew is well worth a visit, with its massive and magnificent rood screen dating from the 15th century. The church is secluded, yet central, with many fine properties and the village school across the encircling path.

KNIGHTSHAYES COURT

Knightshayes Court is located on a south-facing hillside overlooking Tiverton. It was designed by the architect William Burgess whose individualistic approach stands out most clearly in the interiors and in the examples of his furniture which are on view. The house is raised on a great terrace, from which the south gardens can be observed. The grounds extend to woodland walks, but search out the Victorian garden and the water-lily pool. The house is open from March to September, with the gardens and restaurant remaining open until November. Bike racks are available.

Mid-Devon meander

20 miles

Between the mid-Devon market towns of South Molton and Tiverton is a tract of upland country which is bounded by the river Yeo to the south and moorland rising towards Exmoor in the north. This is a part of Devon which rapid transportation links have not reached, and so it has retained its rural pace and charm. There is no drama on this route to pull in the crowds, but instead an enjoyment to be derived from peaceful cycling. Along the way are a number of picturesque villages and hamlets that will delight the eye, and of course the more or less constant backdrop of distant Dartmoor.

Map: OS Landranger 181 Minehead & Brendon Hills (GR 805145) for the start; sheets 180 Barnstaple & Ilfracombe and 191 Okehampton & North Dartmoor are also required to follow the route.

Starting point: The square in the centre of Witheridge to the west of the B3137 South Molton–Tiverton road offers free car parking.

Refreshments: There are shops and pubs (one of which is also a restaurant) in Witheridge, and there are pubs in Morchard Bishop, Black Dog, and Nomansland. There are no cafés on the route.

The route: Most of this route is on the high roads of mid-Devon, with their pleasant shallow gradients. There are two river crossings with hills to follow, neither of which are fearsome. With the exception of two sections of B-road, the route stays in the country lanes, most of which are well surfaced and not too narrow. The ride can be shortened by turning at Puddington for Witheridge, but the shortcut does include an additional river crossing and a steepish climb.

Public Transport: There are no railway stations on the route. However, just two miles into the valley from Morchard Bishop is Morchard Road station on the Exeter to Barnstaple line.

1. Head through the square away from the B-road, keeping **right** into West Street to Drayford Lane. A nice long descent follows out of the village into Drayford. The valley of the Little Dart River stretches out in front; this is the valley that the route follows for the first section of the ride.

At the T-junction **turn R** for East Worlington and Meeshaw and immediately cross the river bridge. To the right is a pleasant shady

Cycling through East Worlington

over your shoulder to see the lovely little thatched cluster of West Worlington hanging onto the hillside above the meandering stream. Eventually the road climbs sharply through the trees to a T-junction (Horsehill Cross); **turn L** for Lapford.

As the hill is crested, the views open out, with Dartmoor to the south and Exmoor to the north. At the T-junction with the B3042 (Tween Moor Cross), **turn R** for Chawley and Eggesford. After a mile **turn L** at the first crossroads (Pouncers Cross) for Lapford. Take care to follow the lane round to the right on a sweeping bend where the give way markings have largely been obscured as a road comes in from the left. On reaching the crossroads (Lower Forches Cross), with just a track opposite, **turn L** for Lapford. At the next junction (Higher Forches Cross) take the **turn to the L** for Eastington and Morchard Bishop.

Across the wide valley ahead is the church tower rising above Morchard Bishop; this is the target. Descend to the River Datch at Calves Bridge. Just before crossing the bridge there is a narrow opening to the right where there is a sheltered spot beside the stream, offering an opportunity to paddle and view the substantial structure of the narrow bridge – a double arch that has been widened in the distant past. Climb up through the trees and on to the top from where

grassy area by the river, complete with seats. At the crossroads (Drayford Cross), **turn L** for Worlington. Following the river in that typical Devon way, the road climbs away from the valley floor to East Worlington. On approaching the T-junction (East Worlington Cross), look out for the old village pump to the right and **turn L** for West Worlington. Descend past the church and primary school to West Worlington. Where the road swings to the right and starts climbing (West Worlington Cross), **turn L** for Milltown. (Continue up the hill to view the church and lychgate.)

2. Drop down and cross the stream to where the road follows the valley floor. Pause and look back

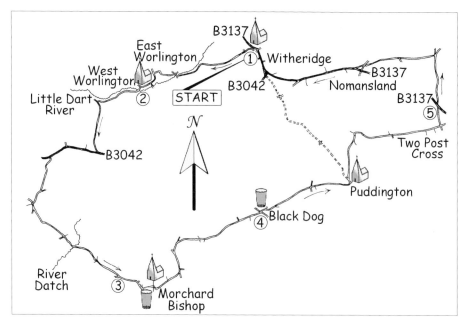

Morchard Bishop can be seen in front. There is first a little dip down to a T-junction (Turningways Cross).

3. **Turn L** for Morchard Bishop. Climb up the main street past the stone cross to **turn L** immediately before the London Inn for Black Dog. The millennium gardens can be seen on the left along this road before the primary school that proudly displays a plaque stating that the politician Ernest Bevin attended school here in 1889.

Follow the road out of the village, past the church. There are a couple of dips along this road but generally it maintains a gentle upwards gradient all the way to Black Dog. Beware, though, for this section of road is the stalking

ground of the Black Dog of myth and legend! For the full story board you will need to enter the wayside pub of the same name, at the crossroads of the same name in the village of the same name.

4. Go **straight over** the crossroads in the direction of Puddington and Tiverton. Ride on through the small village of Puddington. At its end, before the chapel, is a fork to the left for a children's play area, which can then be found on the left.

(For the shortcut to Witheridge, take this **L fork**. Proceed **straight over** the crossroads and cross the steep-sided river valley to join the B3042 for Witheridge.)

Continue down this long and level

road to the first crossroads (Two Post Cross) and **turn L** for Witheridge.

5. At the B-road (Mudford Gate), **turn L** and then immediately **turn R** for Templeton and Rackenford. Take the first **turning L** of the two adjacent left turns (Looseland Cross), signed for Nomansland and Witheridge. Following a small depression for a crossing of a stream, climb up into Nomansland. At the crossroads cross **straight over** for Witheridge. Join the B3137 at a T-junction, **turning R** to ride into Witheridge. As you enter Witheridge the playground can be found on the left. The square is on the left, halfway through the village.

The church spire and gate at West Worlington

EAST AND WEST WORLINGTON

On the south-facing slope of the Little Dart River stand the villages of East and West Worlington, which were linked in 1885 for both civic and ecclesiastical purposes. They are nevertheless very different villages. East Worlington is spread out; at its centre are the church with its squat tower and the school. West Worlington, with its twisted, cedar shingle spire, is a most unusual and attractive place. When viewed across the river valley, it appears as a cluster of thatched roofs with the spire rising from the centre. The church is reached through a lychgate, which is in an arch built into the final cottage of a thatched terrace that rises steeply up the hill.

MORCHARD BISHOP

Morchard Bishop is set on the edge of the uplands of mid-Devon overlooking the Yeo valley, and at the highest point in the village is the church whose tower dominates the village and appears as an important landmark from surrounding hills. Morchard was acquired by the Bishop of Exeter in 1166 and remained in the hands of the church until 1548, when a certain Thomas Darcy bought it. In Fore Street is a terrace of 13 thatched properties; it is said to be the longest thatched terrace in the country and should not be missed.

North-west corner

22, 27, or 35 miles

This route offers glorious diversity: from the charm of the Yeo valley with its hillside estates of Arlington Court and East Hill, to the North Devon coastline, viewed from the gentle undulations of the hilltops, to the magnificent estuary of the river Taw with the Braunton Burrows and marshes, to the historically important town of Barnstaple. It is the longest route in the book, and with so many things to view, admire, and explore you may decide to split the ride over two days, making use of the two circuits which link at the mid-point.

Map: OS Landranger 180 Barnstaple & Ilfracombe (GR 333554).

Starting point: There are various car parks available in Barnstaple, but for this ride the Civic Centre car park is taken as the start. The car park is only available for public use at weekends and there is a charge. The Tarka Trail, which the route starts and finishes on, is to the river side of the car park.

Refreshments: In addition to the large range of eating and drinking places in Barnstaple, there are cafés at Arlington Court and Broomhill Court (should you use the short cut) and commercial diners at Mullacott Cross. There are pubs en route at Clifton, Mullacott Cross, Turnpike Cross, and on the return leg of the Tarka Trail, as well as a garage shop at Lynton Cross.

The route: There are two long climbs: to Arlington Court and to Berry Down. Between the climbs are delightful lanes, mostly in river valleys. The return route involves long easy sections and the final few miles in the Braunton Marshes and on the Tarka Trail is entirely flat. The section on the A3123 can be busy, particularly at weekends in summer.

Public Transport: There is a railway station in Barnstaple, located across the river bridge from the town centre; this is a branch line from Exeter.

1. With the estuary to your right, join and follow the cycle route to the road. **Turn R** to follow the cycle route on the pavement and join the road past the Commercial Road pay-and-display car park, rather than returning to the waterfront. Follow the road round to the left to the T-junction and **turn R**. There is a pedestrian crossing that can be used if the road is busy. Immediately **turn L** into a one-way street and follow it to the T-junction; **turn L**. Follow

The dunes on Braunton Burrows

At the T-junction (Halsey Lake) **turn L** for Luxhore, and at the next T-junction by the phone box (also Halsey Lake) **turn R** for Arlington.

On a right-hand bend just after the horse and carriage sign, **turn L** (White Cawsey Cross) for Arlington. Ignore the turning for Arlington and shortly the car park and gates for Arlington Court will be reached. Cycle parking is available through the gate and next to the visitor's centre.

3. Go down the wide descent to the A39 and **turn L** at the T-junction. Pass the fine old thatched property on the left and descend into the valley. Immediately after crossing the river bridge, **turn R** for East Down. Follow the road round to the left at East Down as it continues to climb.

the road round to the **right** and pass alongside the guildhall on the left. At the T-junction by the Queen's Theatre, **turn L** and then immediately **turn R** into Bear Street. Proceed past Cyril Webber's Cycle Shop to the right and join the road that comes in from the left. Continue to the traffic lights. Cross **straight over** for the steady rise up Bear Street and out of Barnstaple. After passing the cemetery, the road name changes to Goodleigh Road.

2. Take care not to miss the next **L turn**, into a minor road for Luxhore (Luxhore Cross); there is a small grass triangle in the road. Continue to follow the River Yeo until shortly after Luxhore village sign; **turn R** for Lower Luxhore.

4. Follow the lane up to the T-junction (East Down Cross) and **turn R** to pass across the head of the river valley that has been followed all the way from Barnstaple.

(**Turn L** here for a shortcut back to Barnstaple. After a long descent, **turn L** at the T-junction onto the B3230 for Barnstaple. Follow the river valley, past Broomhill Gardens and then up to a T-junction with the A39 (Shirwell Cross); **turn R**. At the traffic lights **turn R** and then **turn L** at the T-junction. **Turn R** just before the river, away from the

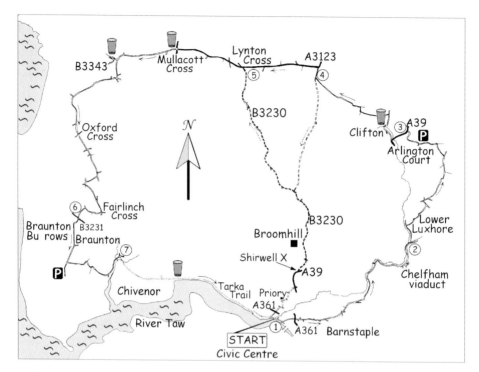

traffic lights. Descend to the A361 and go **straight over** at the traffic lights into Pottington Road. At a sharp bend **keep straight on** down a rough track to join the Tarka Trail from the car park next to the rugby ground. **Turn L** onto the trail and cross the cycle bridge to the Civic Centre car park.)

Drop down to the T-junction with the A3123 and **turn L**. The following few miles are potentially busy, but the views are stupendous on a clear day.

5. At the crossroads (Lynton Cross) there is a garage; **keep straight on** for Woolacombe and Morthoe.

(To ride direct to Lynton Cross, join the cycle route at the Barnstaple Civic Centre with the estuary to the left and cross the cycle bridge. **Turn R** into the rough car park and cross it to join the lane along the east side of the rugby ground. Keep **straight on** into Pottington Road and proceed to the traffic lights, crossing **straight over** the A361 into Fair View Road. **Turn sharp L** just before the traffic lights for Pilton and climb to the left-hand bend; here **turn R** by the priory and follow the road to the traffic lights. **Turn L** and climb to Shirwell Cross and **turn L** for Ilfracombe onto the B3230, following the road all the way up the valley to Lynton Cross.)

At the roundabout cross **straight over** the A361 (Mullacott Cross) onto the B3343. Shortly after, the road swoops round to the right, to Woolacombe. **Fork L** for Croyde into a narrow road. After riding the crest of the hills, the road starts to descend steadily. Immediately after passing under the line of stunted beech and oak trees, take care to **fork L** (Oxford Cross) at a double left turn; it is the second of these turns that the route follows.

At the staggered crossroads (Byecrosspool) cross effectively **straight over**, actually right and then left, signed as cycle route 31. Shortly after a road to the left and just as the road starts to climb, **turn R** into a small lane, there is no signpost.

At the T-junction, **turn L** for Braunton and Orchadon Cross. A fine view over the Taw Estuary and Braunton Burrows can be gained from the vantage point where the lane swings left to follow the edge of the ridge.

Descend sharply to a left-hand bend (Fairlinch Cross) and **turn R** into the first of the two roads to the right. **Turn L** just before the dead-end sign to complete the descent to Braunton Marshes and the main road.

6. Cross **straight over** the B3231 at the staggered crossroads for Braunton Burrows. Ignore the first road to the left but proceed to a long straight, towards the end of which **turn L** into a side road.

(To visit Braunton Burrows, keep straight on to the car park.)

7. At the roundabout **turn R** onto the cyclepath and follow it all the way to Barnstaple. This is the Tarka Trail (see route 18). The first section is alongside Chivenor Aerodrome. There are a couple of emergency gates to cross and the main gates of the air base; care is required here, as it is a difficult crossing to negotiate when there is traffic about. Follow the trail crosses to the modern swing bridge, built for cyclists, the car park is on the opposite side.

• •

ARLINGTON COURT
Arlington Court has been owned by the National Trust since 1947. It had been in the ownership of the Chichester family since the 14th century, although the present house dates from 1822. There is a choice of walks around the grounds. Through the Victorian and walled gardens you can find your way to the stable courtyard, where there is a collection of over 50 carriages displayed in a purpose-built wing.

BRAUNTON BURROWS
This is the largest sand dune system in Great Britain, measuring over four miles long and a mile wide. The dunes reach up to 90 feet high and have an outstanding variety of wildlife and plants. Over 400 different species of flowering plants have been recorded in the dunes.

18
The Tarka Trail and the Yeo valley
24 or 30 miles

Rising through the woods on the old clay line, the Tarka Trail takes you deep into the heart of the Torridge district of Devon before climbing onto the hills contained by the River Torridge as it makes its way round a huge U-bend. From this high ground are fine open views from infrequently used roads. Passing many a field and farm, sections of moorland, woodland, and quiet villages, the route heads out towards the source of the Torridge. The return route finds the deep Yeo river valley, which it follows to the upper tidal reaches of the Torridge. It is here that the Tarka Trail is picked up again for a delightful final run to the pub and café finish.

Map: OS Landranger 180 Barnstaple & Ilfracombe (GR 480197).

Starting point: There is a usefully located car park for the Tarka Trail at the Puffing Billy pub and café, which is situated at the bottom of the hill on the A386, going from Great Torrington in the direction of Bideford. Cycle hire is available at the start.

Refreshments: In addition to the facilities at the start there are pubs at Stibb Cross, Woolfardisworthy (pronounced Woolsery) and Parkham. There are no other cafés on the route.

The route: The first and last sections of this ride climb gently along the Tarka Trail. With the exception of one hill, the route is gently rolling and has no demanding climbs. Apart from a short section of quiet B-road, the route follows cycle routes or country lanes. The lanes vary in width and quality of surface. The Tarka Trail has a good surface downstream of the Puffing Billy, but as it heads south the surface deteriorates if conditions are wet. The ride can be shortened by turning at Powlers Piece for Parkham.

Public Transport: The closest railway station is at Barnstaple, some 12 miles from Landcross on the Tarka Trail, which unfortunately makes it practical only for the fitter cyclist.

---

1. Join the Tarka Trail and head due south under the A386 road bridge and almost immediately over the River Torridge; this is where the line branches away from the river and into the rolling hills. The first road crossing is at Watergate Bridge on the B3227. There is some car parking here, along with picnic tables, if you are in need of an early

The Tarka Trail outside the Puffing Billy café and pub

rest. The surface of the line improves after Watergate.

At the next road crossing (Bagsbeare Halt), leave the trail and **turn R** to start climbing to Berry Cross. There is a bit of a pull at the start but it is really not too strenuous. As the road twists this way and that, passing the entrance to many a farm, enjoy the flowers, which are in abundance in spring. It is clear that this road was more of a link between neighbouring farms than to the more distant towns and villages.

Pass a few short terraces of houses leading to Berry Cross and here go **straight over** for Langtree and Shebear. On the brow of the hill to the left are distant views revealing

the grandeur of the north Dartmoor edge. Pass the old ruined chapel to the right and drop to the T-junction, **turning L** for Langtree and Shebear.

Continue up the rise and over the wooded brow of the hill, **turning R** at the crossroads (Forches Cross) for Langtree and Stibb Cross, and then almost immediately **forking L** on a right-hand bend for Stibb Cross. Follow the lane to the T-junction with the B3227 and **turn L** to climb to Stibb Cross.

2. Ride straight across Stibb Cross, past the pub. Look out for the 'Old Chapel' conversion and **turn R** just before it into a minor road for Woolsery and Clovelly. Enjoy the ride across the crest of the hills,

85

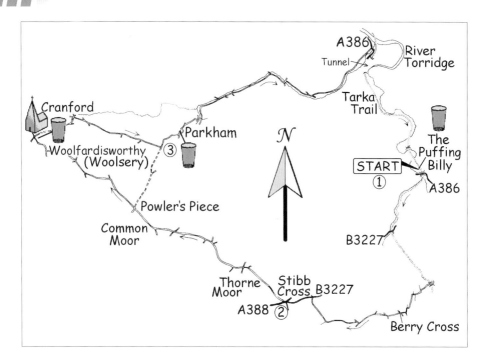

passing various open sections of moorland on the way, each with their own character. Off to the right is the tall mast at Huntshaw, above Torrington; the town can be seen beneath. An open descent leads to a crossroads (Powlers Piece).

(For the short cut to Parkham **turn R** here and then **fork L** at the brow of the hill and rejoin the route at point 3.)

Cross **straight over** for Woolsery and Clovelly and enjoy the fabulous sweep down a beautiful beech-lined road. Proceed with a swing to the right and a swing to the left through the hamlet of Alminstone Cross and on towards the beckoning church of Woolsery.

In true Devon fashion there is a river valley to be crossed first, however.

There is a completely confused arrangement of line markings at the next junction (Lane Hill Cross), but **turn R** here for Woolsery and Clovelly. **Turn R** into the village centre, opposite the primary school, and follow the road through the village and into a dip followed by a short climb. Shortly after the sharp left-hand bend is a crossroads (Cranford Cross); **turn R**. To the left the River Yeo rises, and this river is followed all the way back to the River Torridge. Another fine section follows with the subtle gradient assisting all the way to the next T-junction.

3. **Turn L** here (Copstone Cross) for Parkham and continue the generally descending road into Parkham. At a crossroads opposite the pub cum post office, cross **straight over** into Rectory Lane; then loop to the left and **turn R** at the next T-junction. When passing the church, take care to keep right for Horns Cross into Brewers Lane. There follows a descent with sweeping bends all the way to the crossing of the river Yeo and the T-junction (Parkham Cross); here **turn L** for Bideford.

This road is a favourite amongst cyclists, as it gently descends, following the widening river valley until it becomes tidal. As the estuary opens out, the end of the road is reached at a T-junction at Landcross. (Across the road the river Yeo runs into the wide estuary of the river Torridge.) **Turn R** onto the A386 for Torrington and Okehampton. Cross the river bridge and look out for the cycleway signs. Climb onto the kerb and pass through a gap in the hedge onto the Tarka Trail, **turning R**. This is a descending section; so watch out for fast moving cycles as you ride onto the track.

Climb gently upwards to the tunnel; the apex of the climb is actually halfway through. Thankfully there is low lighting and a good surface through the curving tunnel, which has an unusually steep arch. The canopy of trees which follows will offer decent shelter from a hot sun, if you are lucky, and strong wind. The trail is very definitely heading upstream as it makes its way across three bridges, thus cutting across meanders in the river. At the first bridge there is a locking station for bikes and a signed walk up into the woods, called the Tarka Country Park, to the left of the track. This is a promontory of land bounded by a sweeping bend in the river and the Tarka line. Shortly after the third crossing the welcome site of the Puffing Billy comes into view.

THE TARKA TRAIL

This is the longest off-road cycle route in Devon. It stretches from Braunton, through Barnstaple and Bideford, to Meeth, which is just north of Hatherleigh, a distance of 32 miles. Most of the trail follows the bed of old railway lines which followed the river valleys. The opening of the Tarka Trail has proved what an asset a cycle route can be for the local economy through the influx of tourists. There are now no less than six places along its length to hire a bike. The section used on this route is to the south of Bideford, a railway line that was originally opened to carry clay from the quarries at Meeth and Merton Moors. The further south you go the quieter the line gets as it runs away from the larger rivers and into woodland. Along the way are sidings such as the one at Watergate, which were built to enable local people to use the line, although the majority of users were the workers travelling to the clay workings at Meeth.

87

Towards the source of the Tamar

15 or 23 miles

Rising just a few miles from the Bristol Channel, the river Tamar runs in a southerly direction to the English Channel at Plymouth. Thus Cornwall and Devon had a virtually complete boundary defined by this river. The boundary now deviates from the course of the river in a few locations, but it is no longer fought over, as it was in times past. This route starts in Holsworthy and explores the Devon side of the Tamar. It is necessary to slip in to Cornwall for a mile to reach the Tamar Lakes, a pleasant place to break the ride at mid-distance. Then, crossing back into Devon, the route returns over the higher roads past Holsworthy Beacon, where there are some open views to enjoy.

Map: OS Landranger 190 Bude & Clovelly (GR 344039).

Starting point: The public car park at the northern end of Holsworthy, on the A388. This is a fee paying car park from Monday to Friday and on Saturday morning.Toilets are available nearby, and the town centre is immediately off the car park.

Refreshments: There are cafés at the upper Tamar Lake and in Holsworthy. Pubs can be found in Holsworthy and Pyworthy.

The route: The route is all on minor roads. There are two A-roads to cross, however, and the start and finish of the ride involves a short distance of A-road to enter and leave Holsworthy. Some of the lanes are very narrow, the first section of the ride uses a short distance of a cycle track on an old railway line. Much of the route is generally level, although there are two hills (climbing only 120 to 150 ft), which cross the Tamar valley. There is the opportunity to take a shortcut that misses these hills, but it also misses the Tamar Lakes.

Public Transport: There is no railway station from which this route can be reached but bus X9/X10 between Exeter and Bude, operated by First, will carry bikes at the driver's discretion.

1. **Turn R** out of the car park; then immediately **turn R** again for the town centre, passing under the shadow of the church tower. To visit the town square, take the first road to your right. Otherwise take the next **turning R**, into Bodmin Street, signed to route 3. This is just before the road starts to descend. Ride out of the town, past the

Entering the spiral cycle ramp at Hatherleigh viaduct

unusually grand Methodist church, complete with corner spire, and the Hat Theatre, and go down the hill to the railway viaduct. Cross the road on the crossing with traffic lights to effectively **turn R** to join the cycle track that spirals up onto the viaduct.

Enjoy the views from this elevated cycleway. At the end of the track, you are directed to a bridge by way of a concrete farm track that leads to the minor road. Here **turn R**, thus continuing on route 3.

2. **Turn R** in Pyworthy for Derril and Bridgerule and descend past the Molesworth Arms and the early 14th-century church. Descend out of the village taking care to **fork R**

on the bend where there is a road going straight on. Continue through the hamlet of Derril, staying on route 3. Cross a small bridge; then proceed to the first crossroads and **turn R** for Bridgerule and Holsworthy, now leaving route 3 behind.

Cross the heads of river valleys to both right and left and rise gently to the T-junction, **turning R** for Holsworthy. Eventually the lane leads to the main A3072 at Burnard's House; **turn L** for Bude and then immediately **turn R** for Chilsworthy and Bradworthy.

3. Follow the road to the first **L turn** (Rhude Cross) for Lana; it is shortly after the first right turn.

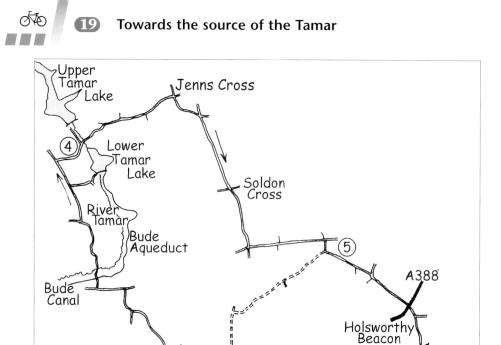

(For the shortcut, ignoring this turning, keep straight on to the T-junction at East Ugworthy Cross and **turn L**. Take the first **R turn** for Honeycroft at West Ugworthy Cross. This lane leads to Honeycroft Cross; here **turn R** to join the route at point 5.)

Follow the lane into a little dip and then back on the level to a T-junction (Gains Cross), to **turn R** for Kilkhampton and Bradworth. At the next T-junction, (Dunsdon Cross) **turn L** for Kilkhampton station. Take the first **turning R** (Broomhill Cross) for Dexbeer and Thurdon.

Descend over the Bude Canal and the river Tamar and then climb the steep hill. After the short wooded section, follow the road around to the right and drop down to cross the border into Cornwall.

(To visit the Lower Tamar Lake, take the first turning to the right and then the first turning left, but watch out for the speed ramps.)

Continue on the lane through Thurdon and past the Tamar Lake campsite to the next **R turn** for Upper Tamar Lake. At the bottom of the dip **turn L** for the Upper Tamar Lake.

4. Returning to the junction, **turn L** and cross the Tamar back into Devon. Climb the long drag which is sheltered by a full canopy of trees. There is a small dip to break the descent, but eventually the top is reached at a crossroads (Jenns Cross); **turn R** for Chilsworthy, Holsworthy, and Sutcombe. Continue to a crossroads and **turn R** for Chilsworthy, Holsworthy, and Sutcombe.

Follow this road for just under two miles, looking out for the second crossroads and here **turning L** for Sutcombe, Milton Dameral, and Youldon Moor Cross.

5. After a mile take the first **turning R**; beware, it is easily missed, as there is no signpost. The shortcut soon comes in from the right on the left-hand bend. Sweep round to the left for Holsworthy Beacon. At the T-junction **turn R** for Holsworthy and Curtis Cross. Follow the gently rising road to the main A388 at Holsworthy Beacon and cross **straight over** for Thornbury and Cookbury. Descend to the first crossroads (Blagdon Moor Cross) and **turn R** for Blagdon Moor Wharf.

Cross the stream and rise up to the edge of Holsworthy, arriving at the A388 alongside the town cemetery (Stanbury Cross); **turn left** for the town centre. Ignore the route 3 sign to the right and proceed **straight over** the roundabout, crossing the A3072, to the car park, which is on the right, just before the church.

● ●

THE TAMAR LAKES

The first of these reservoirs to be constructed was the lower Tamar Lake; in fact, the dam is the oldest in the south-west. It is the smaller and quieter of the two reservoirs and was designated a bird sanctuary in 1951. It offers refuge for more than 50 different species. An observation hide, located to the northern end of the reservoir, can be reached from opposite the road to the upper lake.

Covering 75 acres and holding 300 million gallons, the upper Tamar Lake is in total contrast to the neighbouring reservoir. Overlooking the expanse of water are a visitor centre, a café with indoor and outdoor seating, a shop, toilets, a children's play area, picnic tables, and a water sports training school. There is even a camping field.

20

Okehampton and Dartmoor, Hatherleigh and Torridge

26 miles

etween the two high points of Dartmoor's northern flank, at Okehampton and Hatherleigh moor, is a network of river valleys which feed the river Torridge. These two hills gape at each other across the farmland between and it is in this arena that the route winds its way. The river valleys cut deep into the carboniferous sandstone bedrock in many locations; so the route is chosen with care. Inevitably, though, there are a number of hills. Places of interest are largely restricted to each end of the route, with Meldon viaduct and information centre, Simmons Park, Okehampton Castle and the town centre at one end, and at the other Hatherleigh monument and town centre.

Map: OS Landranger 191 Okehampton & North Dartmoor (GR 593945).

Starting point: The railway station car park but note the time for locking the gates.

Refreshments: Pubs, cafés, and shops can be found in Okehampton and Hatherleigh. There is also a café in a railway carriage at Meldon and a pub as you join the cycleway at Sourton. At Sourton Cross there is a transport café and a Little Chef.

The route: The route is on variable minor roads with the exception of some short linking sections of A- and B-roads around the route. The final section of the route is on a reasonably surfaced Sustrans trail on and alongside an old railway track. There are a few long hills to be ridden, which are concentrated in the middle section of the route.

Public Transport: A seasonal train service operates to Okehampton from Exeter. Bus route 86 between Plymouth and Barnstaple stops at Okehampton, and First, the bus operator, carries bikes.

---

1. **Turn R** out of the car park to descend to Okehampton town centre, **turning R** again at the next T-junction. At the T-junction at the bottom of the hill, **turn R** into Mill Road and pass Symmons Park. This is a pleasant crescent-shaped park beside the River Okement. (To visit the dramatic castle, turn left into Mill Road and then

Meldon viaduct on the Granite Way cycle trail back to Okehampton

immediately left again into Castle Road.)

Turn R at the traffic lights and then immediately **turn sharp L** into a one-way street, Northfield Road. **Turn R** at the T-junction along a short section of cycle route running against the flow of the traffic.

This road becomes the B3217, which initially passes through the industrialised corner of Okehampton but then emerges on a quiet country road following the Okement valley.

Soon after the hamlet of Brightley,

turn **L** for Goldburn by a thatched cottage and cross the River Okement. Enjoy the last of the flood plain while you can, for soon there is the shock of the first hill as the road turns from the river and ascends gently to a crossroads (Coldburn Cross). **Turn R** for Jacobstowe and enjoy the surprisingly long views on a long descent to the river before the small rise in to Jacobstowe.

2. **Turn R** at the T-junction and then immediately **turn L** onto the A3072 for Hatherleigh. Ride around the long bend past the church and old rectory and then **turn R** into a minor road for Cadham. At the T-junction (Terris Cross) **turn L** for Applecot. The level roads give way to an upward gradient, passing through wooded belts; then, where you burst out of the trees, laid out before you is the final climb across Hatherleigh Moor to the monument. At the top of this hill is a T-junction (Deckport Cross), **turn L** for Hatherleigh.

At just under mid-distance, the picnic table here could not be better located. It is blessed with great views across to Dartmoor, where the ride started. The highest hills in the middle are Yes Tor and Higher Willhayes; to the left is Rough Tor, and beneath is the Okement army camp, below which is Okehampton. The tors furthest to the right are the Sourton tors, just beneath which the route joins the Meldon trail to return to Okehampton.

93

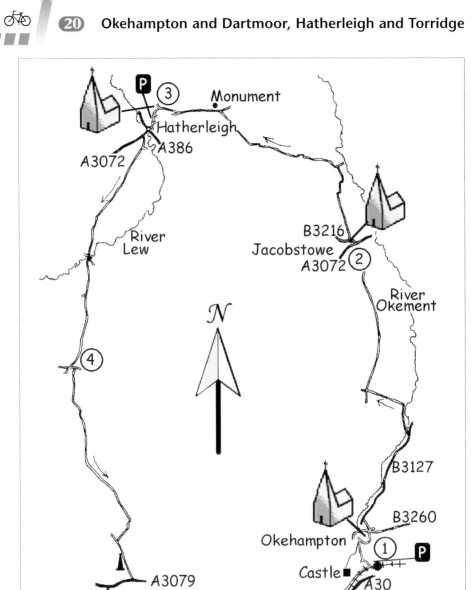

P ③ Monument

Hatherleigh
A386
A3072

River Lew

B3216
Jacobstowe
A3072 ②

River Okement

N

④

B3127

B3260

Okehampton

① P

Castle■ A30

A3079

Cyclepath
Quarry

Transport café
Meldon Viaduct
A30
⑤ Sourton village
Café

Pass the monument to the right and just past the town sign, but before the road descends in to the town, **turn R** into Park Road.

3. **Turn L** at the T-junction to drop down the main street, past the square, and on down to and over the river bridge. Go **straight over** the A386 roundabout onto the A3072 for Holsworthy. **Turn L** almost immediately for Northlew. This is the start of the hilly section of the ride as the route crosses a number of river valleys. After crossing a humpback bridge, the road starts climbing; just after going under the shade of some trees, **fork L** where the road swings to the right at Lambert Cross, signed to Durdon. Soon the steeper slope ebbs away and yet the climb continues all the way up to the crossroads marked by a stone cross.

4. **Turn L** for Okehampton and then take the first **turning R** for Higher Gorhuish and Cruft. (There are great views of Dartmoor now. The chasm which was cut by the Meldon river can be seen clearly; it is spanned by a viaduct that the route will cross later.) This is a long lane that eventually rises up through forestry land and past a golf club to a T-junction (Kigbeare Cross). **Turn L** here for Okehampton and climb up to the mast. Drop down to the T-junction with the A3079 (Ashbury Cross) and **turn R** for Halwill, Holsworthy, and Bude.
After crossing the redundant

railway line, **turn L** into a minor road for Thorndon (Thorndon Cross). Swoop down the long straight, round the bends, over the stream, and then start up the final climb. As the road rises and swings to the right, **turn L** for Okehampton and Cowsen (don't be put off by the name of the junction, Hardhill Cross). The sound of the A30 gets steadily louder; this is good news, as the lane bridges the dual carriageway at the top of the hill. Drop down to the old A30 and turn left for Sourton and Okehampton. Note the old chimney to the right, a relic of the tin mining industry.

5. Drop down to the T-junction with the A386 and **turn R** for Tavistock, Plymouth, and Sourton. Take care as this is a busy section of road. Just after the turning for Sourton village, **turn L** into the access road for Prewley Water Treatment Works. Immediately after crossing the cattle grid, pass through the gate to your left onto the cycleway.

There is now a gentle rise to the brow of the incline at Sourton and then it is downhill almost all the way. It is a great ride: first the crossing of the dramatic viaduct, with its grand views of Dartmoor and the Meldon Viaduct, and then past the open-cast quarry workings. However the path is then relegated to finding its way alongside the railway line and the route zigzags a little but follow the signs and you will be all right. Take care on the occasional sharp bend but look out for views of Okehampton Castle when there is a break in the trees to the left.

As Okehampton Station comes in to view, you are immediately faced with a hairpin, before meeting the road by a granite standing stone. **Turn R** onto the road and follow it down to the crossroads; here cross **straight over** into the station car park.

• •

HATHERLEIGH

Standing on the hill above Hatherleigh is an obelisk commemorating Lieutenant Colonel William Wallace for the part he played in the charge of the Light Brigade in the Battle of Balaclava in 1854. A bronze relief on the obelisk shows him being carried from the battlefield.

The town was given its royal charter in 1693. Halfway up the hill is the town square, behind which is the church, complete with its steeple, rebuilt following its collapse in the gales of January 1990. Opposite is the Tally Ho Inn, with its own brewery off the pub courtyard.

MELDON

The Meldon viaduct is the jewel in the crown for Sustrans, which has successfully opened the line to cyclists, under the name of the Granite Way. The steel viaduct looks like an oversize Meccano model, yet it has towered 150 ft above this ancient industrial valley since 1874, spanning a colossal 165 yards. It is worth pausing to climb down the steps at either

Hatherleigh town square

end of the viaduct and admire the structure beneath the bridge bed. Alongside the viaduct is an old engine shed which now serves as the Dartmoor Railway and Meldon Quarry Visitors' Centre.

OKEHAMPTON

On the edge of Okehampton stands the remains of a Norman castle, with its listing keep. Built on a man-made knoll with a now dry moat on the perimeter, it is an enchanting site and well worth a visit. The Ten Tors challenge, which starts from Okement Camp, the military base that hovers on the moor overlooking Okehampton, is an annual expedition for thousands of teenagers, who walk 35, 45, or 55 miles across the open moor, spending one night under canvas.